CORETTA SCOTT KING
Fighter For Justice

Ruth Turk

BRANDEN PUBLISHING COMPANY
Boston

Library of Congress Cataloging-in-Publication Data

Turk, Ruth, 1917
    Coretta Scott King : fighter for justice / Ruth Turk.
        p.   cm.
    Includes bibliographical references and index.
    Summary: Explores the life and career of Coretta
Scott King, from her childhood in Alabama, through her
work with the civil rights movement, to her continuing
efforts on behalf of the underprivileged.
    ISBN 0-8283-2028-4   (pbk. : alk. Paper)
    1. King, Coretta Scott, 1927- --Juvenile literature. 2.
Afro-American women--Biography--Juvenile literature.
3. Afro-Americans--Biography--Juvenile literature. 4.
Civil rights workers--United States--Biography--Juvenile
literature.   5. Civil rights movements--United States--
History--20th century--Juvenile literature. 6. King,
Martin Luther, Jr., 1929-1968--Juvenile literature. [1.
King, Coretta Scott, 1927- . 2. Civil rights workers. 3.
Afro-Americans--Biography. 4. Women--Biography. 5.
King, Martin Luther, Jr., 1929-1968.] I. Title.
    E185.97.K47T87   1997
    323'.092--dc21
    [B]   96-29786
                                                  CIP
                                                   AC

BRANDEN PUBLISHING COMPANY
17 Station Street
PO Box 843 Brookline Village
Boston, MA 02147

To Len, my husband:
The best research assistant a writer could have.

Coretta *Corrie* Scott
(Courtesy of New England Conservatory of Music).

TABLE OF CONTENTS

Chapter I
DUST IN HER FACE
(1927-1937)

Walking to school three miles every day was quite a trip but young Corrie Scott did not mind because she liked school. What she did mind was watching the school bus filled with laughing, talking white children pass her on the road without slowing down even one bit. As the bus kicked up a thick cloud of gray dust that made her cough, Corrie stole a quick glance at her older sister, Edythe, and her younger brother, Obie. They were staring down at the ground as they walked without saying a word. Corrie realized they felt just as hurt and upset as she did, but she knew they couldn't put it into words. Choking back another cough, Corrie resumed walking but the feelings of misery and hurt did not go away.

Born on April 27, 1927, in a small, all-black community near the town of Heiberger, Alabama, Coretta Scott, called Corrie by her family, did not understand what segregation meant until she was nearly six years old. When she started school she was surprised to discover that the white children's school was in a big brick building separate from the black children's. The school she went to was in an old wooden frame house with one large room where classes were held for more than a hundred children from the first to the sixth grade.

The white children's school had a library and free textbooks for all its students. Corrie's school had no library and very few books. The parents of black children had to pay for some textbooks and other supplies like notebooks and pencils. Instead of regular blackboards some of the walls were painted black so they could be used to write on. A local carpenter had built the combination wooden desks and benches, and the room was heated by a wood-burning stove. When children needed to use the toilet, they had to go outdoors in all kinds of weather to a rickety outhouse.

Once Corrie got inside the classroom, somehow she forgot about the bus and the dust in her face. One reason was her teacher, Mrs. Bennett. When Mrs. Bennett saw that Coretta and Edythe were eager to learn everything, she encouraged them as much as possible. In the early 1930's it wasn't required to have a college education to teach in a black school, but Mrs. Bennett had college training and was very dedicated, especially to pupils who showed a desire to learn.

When Mrs. Bennett also discovered that Corrie had a lovely voice, she called on her to sing solos and lead the class in singing. When the county school supervisor arrived to inspect the school, Mrs. Bennett would arrange for the students to give a special program in which Coretta Scott usually led the singing.

Coretta thought it was unfair for white children to be able to attend school for nine months of the year while black children could only attend for seven. Coretta's mother, Bernice Scott told her daughter that when she was small she could not attend school beyond the fourth grade because her parents needed her to work full time on their farm. She also told Corrie that things would be better for her while she was growing up. Mr.

and Mrs. Scott wanted their children to get the best education possible because they felt that education was the first step on the road to freedom.

"You are just as good as anyone else," Bernice Scott told her daughter. "You get an education and try to be somebody. Then you won't have to be kicked around by anybody, and you won't have to depend on anyone for your livelihood."

As Coretta grew older she kept in mind what her mother told her, but she continued to be upset by the practices of segregation she observed happening all around her. During the 1930's, throughout the south, black people weren't allowed to sit in the front of buses or theaters, eat in the same restaurants as white customers or even drink from the same water fountains.

On Saturdays, sometimes the Scott family would pile into their truck and go shopping in Marion, a town twelve miles away. There Coretta saw signs in the front windows of stores that said, "Whites Only." When she and Edythe tried to buy an ice cream cone in the drugstore, they had to go through a back door. There they had to wait until all the white children were served. When it came her turn, Coretta asked for her favorite flavor but the white store owner gave her the flavor he had too much of. The price was the same he charged the white kids. Coretta would have enjoyed the family visits to Marion, but not being able to try on clothes in a store where whites shopped or have her favorite ice cream was a very frustrating experience.

Fortunately when Coretta got home again, life was much easier to bear. Though the Scotts did not have a lot of money, Coretta's father, Obadiah Scott, owned the farm on which they lived. This was not true for many families in the black community, so the Scotts considered themselves luckier than most. Obadiah Scott was a hard working man who used different skills to improve his family's living conditions. One of his jobs was working in a local sawmill. Mr. Scott taught himself how to be a barber and earned money by cutting people's hair in the evenings. When he saved enough money to buy a truck, Obadiah was able to haul logs and timber for the white mill owner, thus improving his own financial situation.

Whenever they were not in school, the three Scott children helped with chores on the farm. They hoed weeds, picked vegetables, milked the cows, fed the chickens, and drew water from the well. Coretta's mother, Bernice, worked along with them, tending the farm, and cooking nourishing meals for the family. Working in the fields under the hot sun could become pretty tedious but when Corrie started to sing, the others joined in and soon the chores seemed to go that much faster. By working on the farm in this way, the children also managed to save money to help out with the expenses for their school supplies.

In the evenings after all the chores were done, the family would relax on the front porch. There was no television in those times, but Bernice Scott had a few books with nursery rhymes and stories to read to her young ones. There was not much furniture in the simple two-room house but there was one important item which everyone enjoyed and that was the record player or Victrola, as it was called. Coretta, Edythe, and Obie loved to listen to the records their parents played and there was enough variety for everybody's taste, including hymns, popular songs, gospel, and jazz. Coretta would sing her heart out, and the whole family joined in, until the moon went behind the clouds, and it was time to go to bed.

Having a happy home life was a great comfort to Coretta Scott as she was growing up. Another place from which she drew support and much pleasure was the church. Going to church on Sundays was a wonderful social occasion because in this way all the people in the black community got to know each other. Some people came long distances, riding in wagons, or even walking the way Mrs. Scott and her children did when Mr. Scott had to work out of town. Getting dressed up and walking four miles was worth it once they got there and met all their friends and relatives. Coretta had a lot of relatives, including cousins her age, and this was a special day to meet and spend time together. After church there was gossip to exchange and games to play. Young Corrie was not very tall, but she was strong and could outrun and outclimb quite a few kids who were bigger than she was.

Though Coretta was growing constantly more aware of the injustices of segregation, she was, for the most part, protected from severe hardships by her parents. Surrounded by a warm, loving family and a close-knit black community, the young girl did not as yet feel threatened. It was only when her father ran into a dangerous situation with some white men that Coretta Scott began to realize what racial hatred in the South was all about.

Chapter II
HARD TIMES
1937-1942

Because Obadiah Scott was the only black person in the community who owned a truck, a group of white men became jealous and resentful. Though he was a hard worker they thought a black man should not be getting jobs they considered 'belonged' to white workers. In a quiet but determined way, Mr. Scott did his best to ignore these people. He continued working long hours and gradually saved enough money to buy his own sawmill because he wanted to be in business for himself.

One day a white man approached Mr. Scott and offered to buy his sawmill, but Obadiah refused to sell. The other man warned him that he was wasting his time because a black man wasn't supposed to operate his own business. A few nights later the sawmill was burned to the ground. Obadiah could have reported the fire to the police but he knew they would not bother to investigate. Starting all over again, Coretta's father continued to haul lumber and operate a taxi service in addition to being a part-time barber. By 1937, he had saved enough money to move his family into a larger house with six rooms instead of two. There was enough money to buy new furniture for the living room, and Coretta and Edythe were thrilled to have a bedroom all for themselves.

One night on his way home from work, Obadiah was stopped by a crowd of hostile white men brandishing clubs and guns. Shouting and threatening in loud, angry voices they pulled him from his truck. They wanted him to stay in his place like a black man should or else he would be found dead at the bottom of a swamp.

Obadiah felt himself trembling on the inside but he forced himself to wait quietly until the angry crowd had finished. Even though he was tempted to answer, he realized that anything he could say would be used as a reason to attack him. By the time he was able to climb back in his truck and drive away, Obadiah was shaken and exhausted. When he got home late that night, the family knew from the expression on his face that he had gone though a harrowing experience. Mr. Scott didn't want to worry his children, but later when they were alone he told his wife there might be a time, "I may not get back." After this frightening incident, Obadiah bought a gun and carried it in the glove compartment of his truck. He prayed he would never have to use it but he felt more secure knowing it was there.

In 1937 Coretta graduated from the sixth grade at the top of her class. Mrs. Scott wanted her daughters to go to a school that had an excellent reputation in the town of Marion, ten miles away. Lincoln High School had a faculty that was half white and half black, but all the students were black. The white teachers came from the North, but both white and black teachers worked well together because they cared about doing the best job of teaching they knew how for one hundred percent of their pupils. When Mrs. Scott found out about this, she was determined that her children should go there. However, there was more than one problem.

The town of Marion was too far away from the Scott's home to travel back and forth every day, and there was no bus black children could ride. It would also be a sacrifice for Mr. and Mrs. Scott to pay the tuition for three children. Four and half dollars a term for each pupil was a lot of money in those days especially for a family with a limited income. Nevertheless, the Scotts put their heads and hearts together and managed to work things out.

For the first year at Lincoln High, Coretta's mother arranged for her daughters to board with a helpful black family in Marion. For a while Corrie earned part of her expenses by doing housework for a white woman in town. By scrimping and saving every penny they could, the Scotts managed to pay the tuition and board. By the time Coretta was a junior at Lincoln, the county agreed to provide some of the school transportation for rural black students. Mr. Scott bought another truck and when he converted it into a bus, Mrs. Scott drove the black children from their community to and from school every day. Coretta was glad that now she was able to live at home.

Being a student at Lincoln High School became a very rewarding experience for Coretta. From the time she was a little girl she had loved music, and now a whole new world was opening up to her. Recognizing Coretta's musical talent, a dedicated teacher named Olive Williams who was a fine musician herself, gave the young student piano lessons and voice instruction. Before long, Coretta sang in the school chorus and learned to play the trumpet. She and Edythe also sang in a special group called the Lincoln School Little Chorus.

When Coretta was fifteen years old, the church in her community asked her to serve as choir director. She enjoyed training the Junior Choir and doing special programs with them, developing a format which she used years later in her own concerts. Loving music the way she did, Coretta Scott began to dream of a career as a singer. In 1941, the Lincoln School Little Chorus went on a singing tour, performing at several midwestern colleges, among them Antioch College in Yellow Springs, Ohio. This was a wonderful experience for Coretta and Edythe. The following year Antioch College decided to accept black students for the first time. Edythe applied and when she was accepted, Coretta was happy for her.

Though things were going well in school, Coretta was miserable about the strong racial feelings constantly being expressed by white teenagers in Marion. When she walked to school with some of her classmates, a bunch of white students would march down the street and try to push the black students off the sidewalk. Refusing to be thrust into the gutter, the black kids stood their ground. The result was ugly because the white kids called them "dirty niggers," and Coretta and her friends retaliated by calling the others "white trash." It looked like there would be a nasty fight but when Coretta's group moved close together presenting a brave united front, the white group backed off and no blows were exchanged. Coretta felt her heart beat fast, but being with friends gave her the courage she needed to walk away without looking back.

In 1942 on Thanksgiving night, Coretta and Edythe received a very disturbing call. A friend of the family told the girls that their home in Heiberger had been destroyed by fire. Mr. and Mrs. Scott and their son had escaped and were staying with Grandfather McMurry, Bernice Scott's father, but they had nothing but the clothes on their backs. Their nice furniture and all the precious records Coretta had loved listening to as a small girl were now only a pile of ashes. The family home that was the result of years of hard work and sacrifice was gone.

The two sisters felt crushed. Their father was the only black man in the community who had done so well, but he had been continually threatened and warned by those who objected to a black man's success simply because they believed he had "no right." A few sympathetic white people in town advised Obadiah Scott to request an investigation into the cause of the fire, but as before, he felt it would get him nowhere, or even make matters worse. He was glad that at least his family had not been hurt. He also decided to start all over again and rebuild. Coretta was proud of her father's courageous spirit, especially when he insisted that "there are some good white folks." Despite the harassment he received, Obadiah Scott never became bitter or vicious. Listening and watching how her father reacted to these racial attacks, Coretta grew up learning not to hate.

In 1943, Edythe received a full scholarship from Antioch College and became the first black student there. This was an exciting event not only for Edythe, but also for Coretta, because it meant that perhaps there would be an opportunity for her as well. Actually the main attraction for both girls in going to a college in Ohio was the fact that it was far away. To them the idea of leaving the South and going up North meant opening the door to a life free from prejudice and harassment. What Coretta and Edythe did not realize at that time was that there were other problems they would have to face. For now, having the loving support of their parents and the opportunity to achieve a top-rated education up North was all that mattered.

Chapter III
MOVING AHEAD
1942-1951

As soon as Edythe settled into her new routine at college, she wrote letters home describing how great she was finding Antioch. She told Coretta that the college gave students a lot of freedom, and that there were no housemothers or rules about curfew. She was also impressed by that fact that some teachers used the honor system when they gave exams. What delighted Coretta the most was when Edythe wrote that the white students were warm and friendly, and that her sister was sure to love it there.

Later on, Coretta learned that Edythe had left out some of the unfavorable things, because she didn't want to discourage the younger girl. Since Edythe Scott was the first black student to be admitted, she was also in the difficult position of being the first representative of her race at the school. While the students were open and communicative, they seemed to think that Edythe was some sort of authority on race relations. It made her uncomfortable to be constantly questioned especially on occasions when she would rather join in the regular social conversations like everyone else.

Another thing Edythe did not mention in her letters was the fact that, except for one time, she was never asked for a date by any of the young white men on campus. Though she was tall and attractive and the guys found her interesting to talk to, they did not make any romantic moves. The one white student that did ask her out dated her twice before he stopped seeing her. Despite this situation, Edythe felt that the positive aspects of life at Antioch outweighed the negative. As a result she omitted telling Coretta certain things until her sister learned about them for herself.

Focusing on the good things she was told, Coretta became more and more excited about going to Antioch. Since she had achieved excellent grades at Lincoln High, she felt confident about applying for admission to the college. In 1945, Coretta was accepted to Antioch and received a partial scholarship of $450. There were additional fees of $200 plus transportation but her parents provided the money. The new student arrived at Antioch College glowing with anticipation and excitement.

Coretta's first year at college was made easier by the fact that her older sister was still there. Edythe had a quick mind and the ability to express herself effortlessly. At first while Coretta was still shy and inexperienced, her sister would answer questions for her whenever they were too much for the freshman student. By the time Edythe left to spend her senior year at Ohio State college, Coretta was far more responsive and knowledgeable.

As Edythe had reported, Antiochans, as the students at Antioch called themselves, accepted newly arrived students warmly and tried to make them feel at home. Coretta could feel the strong school spirit and wanted very much to be a part of it. She had known that the student body was predominantly white, but not that there were only six black students in the whole school. Coretta's freshman class had two black students besides herself. Edythe's class had two besides Edythe.

Coretta tried hard not to be over sensitive. However, after she had been in Antioch for a while, she began to realize that while the white students were quite friendly, underneath they still felt superior to the black students. She sensed this from the kinds of questions they asked about why black people were loud, or why more black students were not qualified for college. Though sometimes their questions would be prefaced by "Of course, you're different, Corrie," Coretta could not help feeling resentful.

Being a pioneer black student at a predominantly white school in the mid 1940's was not easy, but Coretta Scott was determined to succeed. There were other problems along the way that had to be overcome. Though she had maintained an "A" average in high school, like most black southern students at the time, Coretta was not adequately prepared for college studies. In her second semester she enrolled in a remedial reading course and studied hard, using every spare moment in order to catch up.

As far as social activities were concerned, Coretta knew it was expected she would probably date the one black male student in her class, but the young woman was determined not to give in to this racial assumption. In her junior year, a white student she liked asked her for a date. Because he was a musician and had a good mind, Coretta found they had many interests in common. The two young people saw a lot of each other until Coretta's friend graduated.

One of the things Coretta found very helpful at Antioch was the fact that students there did not place an important value on material possessions, such as clothes. With her limited funds, it would have been a hardship to worry about something like fashion as she might have at another college. The rule at Antioch required all students to combine their studies with employment of some kind. It was part of the curriculum for students to work every other semester and then write a report evaluating their job experience. Among the jobs Coretta held was that of a waitress, a camp counselor, a helper in a nursery school, and a library clerk in several college and public libraries. The job she enjoyed most was working with her father in the general store he opened in 1946, and for which she received credit as part of her job experience. Being able to work while she was going to school was a valuable part of Coretta's education because it taught her not only the skills that the jobs required, but how to get along with different people.

The most frustrating problem Coretta had to face happened when she tried to teach in a public school. It was the first time at Antioch that a black student chose to major in Elementary Education. Education majors were required to teach for a year in the Antioch model elementary school as well as a year in an Ohio public school. For her first year, Coretta chose to teach music at the Antioch school. The experience was a good one because the young student teacher enjoyed her pupils and they enjoyed her. However, the following year things did not turn out very well. When Coretta applied to the School board of Yellow Springs, Ohio for a position to teach, she was turned down. The board members stated that they did not want a black teacher in their public school system. Upset and unhappy, Coretta approached the president of the college and asked him to appeal to the Yellow Springs School Board. She was even more discouraged when the college president told her there was nothing he could do. Coretta got the feeling that he was not strong enough to be a pioneer in race relations.

Later on she heard that the same president had a black dog he called "Nigger."

Finally, the president told her she would have a choice. She could teach another year at the Antioch school or transfer to a segregated black school in another city in Ohio. It was mighty hard for Coretta to accept the fact that she had left Alabama to escape segregation and run into it all over again in the North. Sad and angry by turns, at last she decided to accept a "compromise" for the time being by staying on at Antioch. Coretta did not think it was the right thing but she believed it was the only thing she could do right then. She was also determined not to let the troubling situation get her down so that she could so something about it in the future for students who came after her.

Soon after this incident, Coretta joined the NAACP (National Association for the Advancement of Colored People), a Civil Liberties Committee, and a Race Relations Committee. Each of these organizations had chapters on the Antioch campus and Coretta became involved with many of their activities. The purpose of these groups was to promote the rights of all people, no matter what race they came from.

Despite her unfortunate experience, Coretta managed to continue her serious study of music. She considered herself lucky to be in the classes of one of the most popular and talented professors in the school. Dr. Walter Anderson was the head of Antioch's Music Department, and at the time, was also the school's only black faculty member. When Coretta started preparing for her first public concert, Dr. Anderson coached her.

In 1948, at the Second Baptist Church in Springfield, Ohio, Coretta Scott made her singing debut and was enthusiastically received. After that she performed in other concerts, appearing on one occasion on a program with the famous black singer, Paul Robeson. Afterwards Mr. Robeson encouraged her to continue developing her talent because he felt she had excellent potential to become a fine singer.

At school Coretta's counselors also suggested that she should continue with her voice training at a professional conservatory of music. Dr. Anderson advised that she should go to New York or Boston where some of the best conservatories were located. Coretta applied to the Julliard School in New York and the New England Conservatory of Music in Boston. When she was accepted by the New England Conservatory, she was delighted because Boston had been her first choice. She thought that life in New York might be too impersonal and competitive for a struggling student. Boston might be less hectic but still offer the cultural opportunities she was seeking.

In 1951 Coretta graduated from Antioch College. Because she needed financial aid to pay her tuition and expenses, Coretta applied for several grants and scholarships. The only reply she received came from the Jessie Smith Noyes Foundation but it informed her that their grants were completely filled for the following year. However, they added that if a chosen applicant decided not to use the grant, it would then be given to Coretta Scott. Of course this was not of much consolation for the young woman, but it was better than nothing.

Coretta knew her parents would help her out, but she felt she had been dependent on them long enough. She made up her mind she would go to Boston, whether or not a scholarship came through. She felt she could always get a job and attend school part time even if it meant her studies would take longer to complete. With only enough money for train fare and fifteen dollars for expenses, Coretta left for Boston.

When the train made a stop in New York she called her parents. They told her there was a letter from the Noyes Foundation. Heart beating fast she listened while her mother opened the letter and read its contents over the phone. Coretta Scott had been awarded a $650 grant to study at the New England Conservatory of Music.

It was a dream come true.

Chapter IV
MARTIN
1951-1955

Coretta's first days in Boston were difficult. She went to live in the Beacon Hill home of a lady named Mrs. Bartol who rented rooms to students. Though the cost for a room and breakfast was a reasonable seven dollars a week, Coretta's grant was only enough to pay for tuition and fees. The fifteen dollars she had when she arrived was almost gone. Coretta had refused to accept a regular allowance from her parents but Mrs. Scott said she would send money from time to time. So far, no money had arrived and Coretta was almost out of funds.

Determined to study full-time at the conservatory, the young student realized she would need to find a job to pay for her board. One time Coretta found she had only twenty-five cents for her carfare back from the conservatory but at least it got her there. That night her dinner consisted of graham crackers and peanut butter. The next morning Coretta asked Mrs. Bartol if she could do some housework for her so she could pay for her board. Mrs. Bartol already had a cook and two maids but she agreed to let Coretta help with some of the housework. The landlady arranged for the young woman to clean her own room and two other bedrooms on the fifth floor. She also had to clean the hallways and a long staircase that led from the fifth floor. Mrs. Bartol wanted a thorough job done and the two Irish maids showed the new worker how to scrub the floors the way they did on their hands and knees.

Coretta was glad that the housework paid for her room and breakfast, but she still needed money for her other meals and a few extras. She succeeded in persuading the landlady to pay her for washing the towels and pillowcases on Saturdays. Fortunately, Coretta did not have to do this work too long. The Urban League found her a part-time job with a mail order company, and some money also arrived from home.

The next semester Coretta received an unexpected grant from the state of Alabama. Because the state chose to maintain segregated schools, they made grants to black students who wanted professional training for which there were no facilities in Alabama's black colleges. Coretta didn't mind what the state's reason was. Developing her voice was the most important thing in her life at that time. Anything that would allow her the opportunity to advance her music studies was most welcome. A short time later when the New England Conservatory itself awarded her an additional hundred dollar scholarship, she felt she was probably the happiest student in the entire school.

Whatever social life Coretta managed to have was involved with a small group of black students at the conservatory. There was only a limited number of black students in the Boston area, a fact Coretta soon learned. Though there weren't any "No Whites Only" signs posted, black women and men did not feel comfortable eating in white restaurants. As a result most black young people met in private homes or in the few southern-style restaurants that welcomed black customers. One such restaurant, the Western Lunch Box, was near the conservatory but Coretta could not get there frequently because Mrs. Bartol's boarding house was too far away.

Some of the black students dated each other but Coretta was not interested in acquiring a boyfriend. She was very serious about her studies and her goal as a concert singer. Though she had a strong belief in God, when she first came to Boston she did not attend church regularly. As the only black person living in the Beacon Hill area, Coretta did not want to attend services in an all-white church. Instead she decided to worship in her own room.

One of the conservatory students who became a friend of Coretta's was named Mary Powell. Though she was older than Coretta and married, the two young women were attracted to each other because they had similar backgrounds and interests. Another reason they became friendly was that there were very few black women studying at the conservatory.

What Coretta did not know about her friend was that she enjoyed doing a bit of matchmaking whenever a likely occasion arose. She found out about this one day when Mary told Coretta she would like her to meet a young preacher that she knew. Though Mary assured her that he was a very promising young man who was studying for his doctorate at Boston University, Coretta said she was not interested. To start with she was not ready for a serious date, and secondly, the idea of a minister was not at all appealing. Coretta's mind imagined the stereotypes of ministers she had known who were very conservative and narrow-minded in their beliefs. What made it worse was the fact that the young man was a Baptist minister. Coretta knew that Baptists believed you had to be immersed in water to be baptized and have your soul saved. In the church to which Coretta and her parents belonged, the practice of sprinkling water on a person was considered adequate for baptism. The idea of baptism by immersion was a negative image in Coretta's mind.

Nevertheless, a few days later Coretta received a phone call from someone who introduced himself as a friend of Mary Powell. He told her his name was Martin Luther King, Jr. and he would like to meet her. The voice was pleasant and most persuasive and before she realized what was happening, Coretta was enjoying her conversation with a stranger. They talked mostly about each other's studies and reasons for being in Boston. Before he hung up, Martin convinced Coretta to meet him for lunch the next day. Coretta told herself it could not hurt to see him just this once.

The next day was cold and rainy. Coretta pulled a scarf over her long dark hair and buttoned her coat up to her neck. They had arranged to meet outside one of the conservatory buildings because Coretta was free from twelve to one between classes. As an old green Chevy pulled up to the curb, she could see what appeared to be a very short, ordinary looking man sitting at the wheel. Hiding her disappointment she got into the car and tried to be polite. Martin drove to a restaurant on Massachusetts Avenue where they ate lunch, cafeteria style. By the time the meal was over, Coretta had completely revised her first impression. As he looked intently into her eyes across the table and spoke to her, Coretta's lunch companion seemed to grow taller and better-looking by the minute. The deep, compelling voice, the warm manner, and animated language, were more attractive than Coretta could have imagined.

As for Martin, he made no pretense of concealing how he felt about his blind date. His gaze did not leave her smooth honey-colored skin or silky black hair falling around her shoulders. As he drove Coretta back to her class, the young man said something that left her almost breathless.

"You have everything I have ever wanted in a wife. There are only four things, and you have them all."

Flustered but curious the young woman answered.

"I don't see how you can say that. You don't even know me."

"Yes, I can tell," Martin came back. "The four things that I look for in a wife are character, intelligence, personality and beauty. And you have them all. I want to see you again. When can I?"

It was difficult for Coretta to maintain her poise, but she recovered quickly and told her companion she didn't know, but that he could call her later.

Back in her room, Coretta realized she had been very moved by her meeting with Martin Luther King, Jr. She did not want anyone or anything to stop her on her way to her career, but she also knew she would see Martin again. She tried to reassure herself that he couldn't possibly mean what he had said about marriage, that surely he must have been joking. Soon Coretta learned that she was wrong. The next day Martin called to ask if she could see him Saturday night. Coretta told him she had a tentative date for Saturday with someone who was to escort her to a party at a friend's house. If by some chance the young man could not make it, if Martin were agreeable, he could take her. Martin was agreeable. He was also delighted when it turned out that the other man could not make it. Martin escorted Coretta to the party and received a lot of attention, especially from some of the young women guests. They all seemed to have heard of the dynamic minister who was also the most eligible bachelor in the black community of Boston. Though Martin did not neglect Coretta, he appeared pleased with being the center of attention and charmed everyone within listening distance. Observing what was happening, Coretta tried to act calm and poised. She realized she had no claim on her escort, but in her heart she was beginning to wish she had.

From that time on, the relationship between Coretta and Martin started to deepen. They spent quality time together talking about her interest in music and his interest in philosophy. Martin would also talk about the problems faced by black people and how he wished one day they would be free from oppression. On Sundays Coretta would attend the Baptist Church in Roxbury to hear Martin preach. A few times she was asked to sing for the congregation and enjoyed the warm applause she received.

There was a fun side to Martin was well as his serious side. When he was not listening to music, he loved to dance. At parties the young couple did a lot of dancing. On one of their dates, Martin took Coretta to a concert as Boston's Symphony Hall, a place she could not have afforded on her tiny budget. Coretta was aware she was coming to care for Martin more and more, but she was apprehensive about making a commitment. The notion of being a Baptist minister's wife still did not appeal to her. One day she discussed her feelings with her sister, Edythe. After meeting Martin, Edythe simply advised Coretta to marry him. By this time, Coretta did not need any prompting. She knew her heart had decided the problem for her.

Martin believed that women were as capable and intelligent as men and could hold important positions. However, this attitude was combined with the belief that his wife should be a homemaker and the mother of future children. Even while she was falling in love, Coretta was concerned about whether she could combine a singing career with the roles of a wife and mother. She was also not sure that Martin's parents would approve of his choice of a wife. Martin had confided that Mr. and Mrs. King, Senior had picked out another girl for him some time ago, but he did not love her.

In November, 1952, Martin introduced Coretta to his parents when they came on a visit to Boston. When they saw how serious their son was about the pretty young woman, they had no choice but to give the couple their blessing.

On June 18, 1953, Coretta and Martin were married on the lawn of the Scott's new home built by Obadiah Scott next to his general store outside of Marion, Alabama. Bypassing the tradition of a formal white wedding gown, Coretta wore a pale blue lace dress with matching gloves and shoes. Edythe and the family had decorated the wedding arch with vines and flowers from the Scott's garden and a delightful fragrance filled the air. Because the couple had requested it, the part of the marriage vows where the bride promises to obey was left out. Coretta and Martin were determined to be equal partners in their life together.

Coretta King
New England Conservatory Commencement
(Photo by Frederick G. S. Clow)

An aspiring Coretta King
at New England Conservatory of Music.
(Courtesy of New England Conservatory of Music).

Chapter V
AN INCIDENT IN MONTGOMERY
1955-1962

Segregation laws in the South did not allow black couples to check into a hotel for any reason even if they were just married, but the Kings were happy to spend their wedding night at a friend's home in Marion. The next day they drove back to Atlanta where Coretta's in-laws gave a reception for Martin's friends.

During the summer, Martin worked with his father, *Daddy King* as he was called, who was the pastor of Ebenezer Baptist Church. Serving as assistant pastor was valuable experience for the young man, especially since the church had a congregation of several thousand members. In September, Coretta and Martin returned to Boston. There they rented their first apartment together, shared in the household duties, and continued with their studies.

It was a happy year for the newlyweds as well as a busy one. In order to complete her degree Coretta took thirteen credits in one semester. Along with classes in choir directing, orchestral arrangement and directing, voice, piano, brass, percussion, strings and woodwinds, she also had to do practice teaching. Coretta was the only black student teacher in the Boston public schools, but there was no problem as there had been in Ohio. Her pupils loved her and her superiors gave her an excellent rating for teaching.

While Coretta moved from one activity to another, Martin was busy working on his doctoral thesis, attending classes, and occasionally preaching at local Baptist churches. On Saturdays they did the weekly grocery shopping and sometimes Martin did the cooking. Soul food was a favorite with both young people. When it was his turn, Martin enjoyed preparing a delicious meal of smothered cabbage with pork chops or fried chicken and turnip greens, southern style, with ham hocks and bacon drippings, only cheating on the cornbread for which he bought a mix.

When Coretta received her bachelor's degree in music education, her mother and Martin were proud spectators in the conservatory auditorium. In the spring of 1954, Martin received several invitations from black Baptist churches looking for a new pastor. The prospective candidate would give a sermon to the congregation and if the members liked him, the offer of a position would be made soon after. In March, Martin received an offer to become pastor of the Dexter Avenue Baptist Church in Montgomery, Alabama.

Martin and Coretta had made friends in the Boston area and they liked their lifestyle. Coretta also planned to take up a music career there. Leaving behind a comfortable life with people and things they knew was a difficult decision to make. They also felt there was less obvious segregation and more opportunity for advancement in the North. For the next few days the young couple discussed the issues back and forth. They also thought and prayed a lot.

Coretta wanted to return to the South someday but she was not prepared to go just yet. Then something happened which helped to change the young woman's mind.

On May 17, 1954, the United States Supreme Court ruled that segregation in the public schools was unconstitutional. Martin and Coretta felt this was a significant event in the lives of black people. They agreed that returning to their roots at that time would allow Martin to do the most good in the black community.

On a Sunday in July, 1954, Coretta and Martin arrived at the Dexter Avenue Baptist Church. After the new pastor spoke to the congregation, Martin introduced his wife. Though she was nervous, with Martin's encouragement, Coretta smiled and said a few words. She thanked the members for inviting Martin to be their pastor and asked for their prayers in helping her to become a dedicated minister's wife. After the service, the Kings were escorted to see the house where the pastor and his family would be living. Located on South Jackson Street, less than a mile from the church, the parsonage was a large wooden house with seven rooms and a porch. The outside looked somewhat run-down but on the inside there was plenty of comfortable furniture. The church members offered to redecorate the house to suit the new occupant's taste, but Coretta thought it wasn't necessary. Now that she had met the congregation and seen how warmly they received Martin, she felt more positive about settling in Montgomery. At the beginning she had been reluctant but now she started to realize "that it was an inevitable part of a greater plan for our lives. Even in 1954 I felt that my husband was being prepared, and I, too, for a special role about which we would learn more later."

In that first year in Montgomery, Coretta's role was mostly home-centered. Singing in the church choir, appearing in local concerts, helping Martin with secretarial chores and keeping house, occupied most of her days. Martin spent long hours preparing his sermons, attending committee meetings, performing marriages, conducting funeral services, and making visits to members of his church. The Dexter Avenue Church had a congregation composed mostly of middle-class, well-educated black men and women who held different jobs at the local college for African Americans. Martin was glad that many members were affiliated with Alabama State College, but he also wanted less advantaged people to feel welcome at his church. He joined the NAACP (National Association for the Advancement of Colored People) and was invited to serve on the local executive committee. He also became involved with the Alabama Council for Human Rights which was the only interracial organization in the city.

Among the friends Coretta and Martin made in Montgomery was a young couple named Juanita and Ralph Abernathy. Rev. Abernathy was a pastor at another church. The two women had a lot in common because they were about the same age and both were college graduates, a unique achievement for black people of either sex in the South in the 50's. Since they couldn't go out to restaurants, they alternated preparing dinners at home and talked about segregation and other racial problems. Like the Kings, the Abernathys were committed to social reforms so there was lots to talk about.

In the spring of 1955, Coretta and Martin celebrated two joyful events. Martin was awarded his Ph. D. in theology and Coretta learned that she was pregnant. On November 17th, the King's first child was born. They named their little daughter, Yolanda Denise, but soon gave her the nickname of *Yoki*.

Being a family made Martin and Coretta feel warm and fulfilled. Life seemed pretty calm and peaceful until one day, a few weeks later. On December 1, 1955, an incident occurred in Montgomery that changed the entire direction of their lives.

On December first, a black seamstress named Rosa Parks boarded a bus on her way home from work in downtown Montgomery. She had been working hard and was feeling quite tired. Moving to the section behind the last row of "whites only" she sat down in an empty seat. In a few minutes, all the white seats filled up. Turning around, the bus driver ordered Mrs. Parks to give her seat to a white man who was standing. Mrs. Parks was a small, forty-two year old woman with a gentle personality. That night she was not feeling rebellious, just plain exhausted. Suddenly the thought of having to stand on her aching feet all the way home was too much for her. Shaking her head, she refused to give up her seat. Without hesitating a moment the bus driver called a policeman. When the policeman told her to stand, Mrs. Parks asked him why, but all he said was that he was following the law. As black and white passengers watched, Rosa Parks was handcuffed, arrested and removed from the bus.

In the courthouse Mrs. Parks called E. D. Nixon, a black community leader for whom she had once worked as a secretary. Mr. Nixon came down and signed a bail bond for her release, but he was angry and upset. He told her, if she would agree, he would like to use her case to try to end segregation on the buses in Montgomery. Rosa Parks agreed. Within minutes, phones all over the black community started to ring. Contacting all the black ministers and business men in the city, Nixon invited them to meet to plan an all-out protest against the treatment of black passengers on Montgomery buses.

Early in the morning of Friday, December 2nd, Nixon called Martin Luther King, Jr. When he heard the story, Martin immediately offered the Dexter Avenue Baptist church as a meeting place. A meeting was arranged for the same night and more calls went out. Martin wondered how many leaders would turn up, but as he entered his church that evening he found a large crowd of people from all walks of black life. Not only businessmen and ministers, but doctors, lawyers, federal government employees and union leaders had turned out. After a long hectic meeting an unanimous decision was reached. It was agreed that everyone in the black community would be asked to join a one-day boycott of buses in the city of Montgomery. The date was set for Monday, December 5th.

On Sunday, the day before, the city's black ministers made the announcement from their pulpits. That night members of the Women's Political Council worked for hours running off 52,000 flyers asking the black community not to ride the buses on Monday. While Coretta stayed home answering calls, Martin rode all over town asking black cab and car owners to offer special fares and rides to protesters. In the past other black leaders had attempted protests but none of them had been successful. Martin and Coretta were worried that this one would fail, too.

The next morning the anxious couple rose at 5:30, dressed and had some coffee and toast. The first bus was due at 6 o'clock at the bus stop outside their house, but they could hardly wait. Would the bus be full or empty? Exactly on schedule, the bus came down the street, headlights shining through the December gloom.

Inside the bus, the only person in sight was the driver. Too excited to believe what was happening, the two people remained at the window to watch for another bus. Not only was the next bus empty, but so was every bus that came along.

Martin called for his friend Ralph Abernathy and the two men drove around the city. It was the same everywhere. With the exception of a few white and one or two black people, the buses in Montgomery were silent and empty. All along the streets groups of men and women were walking to work. Some people rode on mules while others drove horse drawn buggies. There was no doubt about it -- the boycott was a success. Black people in Montgomery had been mistreated for a long time but finally by uniting on this day, they had been able to show how they felt.

That evening a large group of community leaders got together and formed the Montgomery Improvement Association. Martin had been invited to the meeting but was a little late getting there. As he entered the hall, he was told that he had been elected president. Martin knew that this was a dangerous post because it meant he could become the target of white people's anger and retaliation. Yet, when he was asked if he would accept, he answered, "I don't mind. Somebody has to do it, and if you think I can, I will serve." Martin was nervous about telling Coretta of his new responsibility but when he did, her reply was, "You know that whatever you do, you have my backing."

To begin with, Martin and the other members of the M.I.A. tried to reason with the bus company and city officials to change their policy on segregation, but they refused. The M.I.A. then voted to continue the bus boycott. Martin felt they had no alternative except to protest, but he urged that their best "weapon of protest" would be non-violent resistance. Martin had studied the principles of Mahatma Ghandi, a strong leader from India, who had led his country to independence by the use of non-violent action.

More than 50,000 black residents of Montgomery listened to Martin and, under his guidance, agreed to continue a peaceful boycott. For the next eleven months and eight days, the black residents of the city walked in the rain, the heat, and the cold. Special meetings were held in churches around the city to help keep their spirits up. A motor pool of volunteer drivers was organized and soon there were over three hundred cars participating. Without meaning to, some white women helped by driving to pick up their black maids to make certain they got to work.

Though Coretta was busy taking care of her baby, she played an important role by running the office of the M.I.A. in their home. All day long the phone kept ringing and groups of people turned up in their living room for meetings. Coretta never knew how many would stay for dinner, but somehow she always managed to feed them. Every day a number of reporters would be waiting for Martin to get home so they could interview him.

By now, newspapers and radio and TV stations around the country had become interested and were starting to report what was happening in Montgomery. Organizations and churches invited Martin to speak and he accepted in order to raise money for the growing movement. Coretta and Martin began receiving abusive calls and threats; but while this troubled them, it did not deter them. When the calls became more frequent, the Kings decided to move their sleeping quarters to the back of the house because the front of the house faced the street and was more accessible. The back was surrounded by a deep yard enclosed with a high fence which offered better protection.

On Monday, January 30, 1956, Coretta was in the living room talking with a friend. Suddenly there was a loud noise on the porch. Coretta quickly grabbed little Yoki who was playing nearby and she and her visitor ran to the back of the house. A moment later there was a deafening explosion, followed by the sound of breaking glass and wood. A bomb had split the front porch and blown a deep hole in the floor. Fortunately no one was hurt but Coretta was badly shaken. She tried to be brave about it but she also realized that her family was in a very dangerous situation. After lengthy discussion, the Kings still felt they had no choice. Too many people were now looking up to Martin as a strong leader and Coretta as his most valued helper. Deciding that they were needed by the community, they had the house repaired, installed floodlights front and back, and the church hired a watchman to protect the premises.

On November 13, 1956, the United States Supreme Court ruled that segregated buses were unconstitutional. At last black passengers had the right to sit anywhere a seat was empty on any bus. The boycott in Montgomery was called off, but many whites reacted violently to the court decision. The Abernathy's home and church were among some of the black-owned buildings that were bombed, as was the home of E.D. Nixon.

Even after the frightening attack on her home and family, Coretta did not regret their decision to remain in Montgomery. Though the boycott was over, the M.I.A. continued its work. In order to raise money for the association, a number of black leaders who were involved with the civil rights movement planned a big concert at the Manhattan Center in New York. On December 5, 1956, the first anniversary of the boycott, several great performers including folk singer Harry Belafonte and jazz musician Duke Ellington, were invited to entertain. Another star on the program was Coretta Scott King.

Dressed in a glamorous white evening gown, she sang a selection of classical songs. As the full house listened spellbound, Coretta then proceeded to tell the story of the Montgomery boycott using words and music as she used to do when she was in Lincoln High School. Following her narration, she sang the spirituals the people sang to give them moral support as they walked to work because they would not use the buses. She completed her performance by singing Martin's favorite spiritual, "Honor, Honor."

It was at this concert that the Kings met Harry Belafonte who was to become one of their closest friends, and who was always there for them in the years that followed.

When the Kings returned to Montgomery, there was still another eruption of violence. Bombs were tossed and a pile of dynamite was found smoldering on their new front porch. Finally the city authorities took a firm stand. Strong editorials in the press and statements by white ministers urged desegregation without violence. An organization of white business men stated they were opposed to the bombing of black homes and churches. As the leading white citizens began to speak out, Martin began to feel they had received the message of non-violence at last. He was very thankful that not one person had died as a result of the Montgomery Freedom Movement.

As news of the successful boycott spread to other cities, thousands of black people were encouraged to negotiate for their rights. Many of them called on Martin to help them mobilize. Coretta was aware that her husband had become a hero to black people all over the United States. The Civil Rights Movement had opened a new and vital era of social change. Martin Luther King Jr. was now its leader and Coretta Scott King had become his most important partner and helper.

Chapter VI
THE CIVIL RIGHTS MOVEMENT
1962-1972

As more and more black leaders in other cities continued to contact Martin, he realized the need for a central organization to mobilize the movement for civil rights. After many discussions held mostly in the King's home, plans were finalized in December, 1956. A conference of black leaders was scheduled to meet in Atlanta on January 10, 1957.

Coretta, Martin, and little Yoki arrived in Atlanta the day before so they could spend some time with Martin's family. Ralph Abernathy traveled with them because he wanted to attend the meeting. Suddenly at two o'clock in the morning, Ralph received an alarming call. His wife, Juanita, told him their house had been bombed, but fortunately she and the children had escaped unharmed. Even though his family was safe, Ralph wanted to return to Montgomery at once and Martin decided to go with him. An important meeting was scheduled for the morning and he was expected to run it, but Martin felt he was needed in Montgomery. When he asked Coretta to take over for him, she did not hesitate.

The next day when the meeting was called to order, Coretta was the first speaker. Talking in a low, steady voice she explained why Martin was unable to be present and about the violence in Montgomery. Then she presented the agenda for the meeting. It was unanimously accepted and the meeting proceeded as planned.

When Martin returned to Atlanta the next day, he was exhausted but the warm reception of the people at the conference helped to make him feel better. Under his leadership, an organization called the Southern Christian Leadership Conference (or SCLC) was formed and offices were set up in Atlanta because it was a major city in the South.

In February, 1957, *Time Magazine* ran a feature story on Martin Luther King, Jr. in which they described him as "the scholarly Negro Baptist minister who in little more than a year, has risen from nowhere to become one of the nation's remarkable leaders of men." Included with the story was a picture of Coretta and their daughter Yolanda with a caption that read, "They earned their right to the name."

It was not long before people around the world were reading about Martin and the struggle for racial equality in the South. In another part of the world, the African country of Ghana, a former British colony, had just won its independence from England. When the Kings received an invitation from Kwame Nkrumah, the head of the new government, to be present at the Independence Day ceremonies in Ghana, they were thrilled and excited. Nkrumah was an African who had been educated in the United States and he wanted Martin to come to Ghana. On his part, Martin had always felt there was a close relationship between the black struggle in the South and the black struggle in Africa.

Both he and Coretta wanted more than anything to accept the invitation, but there was a problem.

Though the Kings would be guests of the Ghana government, they could not afford to pay their airfare and other expenses. However, as soon as the congregation of the Dexter Avenue Church learned about the situation, they immediately came to the rescue. Contributions from both the church and the M.I.A. made it possible for Coretta and Martin to make the trip. Both these groups felt it would be a valuable experience for the black leader because it meant he would be able to contribute even more to the life of the church and the community.

On March 3, 1957, Coretta, Martin, and several other black leaders boarded the plane for Africa. Representatives of 68 nations attended the ceremony, among them Vice-president Richard Nixon representing the United States. In the capital city of Accra, Coretta and Martin were driven to Achinmota College where they stayed with an English professor and his wife. In a low stucco bungalow they slept on cots with thin mattresses and no springs. These accommodations were quite different from those of a typical American college, but Coretta observed another difference that really upset her. At breakfast there were a number of servants who waited on them continuously. On learning they were paid 28 cents a day, the Kings were shocked. It was also disturbing to see how the serving people always kept bowing low, almost as if they were cringing rather than just being polite. Everyone in Accra seemed to have servants and they all behaved the same way.

Having heard that Africa was a primitive continent, the Americans were unprepared for the handsome streets and luxurious government-owned Hotel Ambassador to which they were escorted. During the next few days, Coretta and Martin witnessed a great deal of pomp and ceremony. The outstanding event occurred at midnight on March 6th. While the bells rang out the British flag was lowered and the new flag of Ghana was raised in its place. As the green flag rippled in the evening breeze, there was wild cheering from 50,000 Ghanaians crowded together in the square. They continued to cheer when Nkrumah, wearing the splendid robes of his Akan tribe, ascended the raised platform. As the bells began to toll midnight, the black leader raised this hand and the people listened.

In English he said, "At long last the battle has ended. Ghana, our beloved country, is free forever. Let us pause one minute to give thanks to almighty God." The crowd fell silent. At the end of a minute, there was a mighty roar as 50,000 voices joined in lifting their voices. "Ghana is free; Ghana is free." For Coretta and Martin it was an immensely thrilling moment. Watching the Ghanaian people celebrate their freedom made them proud of their African heritage. They also felt that Ghana was a symbol of the hopes and aspirations of black people everywhere.

After leaving Ghana, the Kings traveled to Nigeria, Rome, Geneva, Paris, and London. They had never been to any of these places and it was a rewarding experience. Everywhere they went they were welcomed and entertained by officials from the United States embassies. On their return to the United States, Martin was awarded the Spingarn Medal given by the NAACP to the person who made the greatest contribution to race relations in the previous year. When Martin's *alma mater* Morehouse College recognized him by presenting him with an honorary degree, Coretta was proud and delighted. She was also proud and delighted to find that she was expecting another child.

Now that they were back in Montgomery, the young couple was caught up once more in a whirl of civil rights activities. Because Martin realized that President Eisenhower was not moving ahead with the important matter of black voting rights, hc felt it was time to do something about it. For a long time, black citizens had been prevented from voting in local or national elections. After a number of conferences with other black leaders, it was decided to organize a march to Washington, D. C. in order to motivate the passage of new civil rights legislation. Wanting to emphasize the nonviolent nature of this demonstration, Martin called the march a Prayer Pilgrimage for Freedom. Since the walk was less than a mile, even though Coretta was pregnant, she wanted to participate. However, when Martin urged his wife not to because of her condition, she agreed to stay at home but she was not happy about it. There were occasions when Coretta did not feel the same way her husband did, but she always remained loyal and usually abided by his wishes.

On May 17, 1957, 37,000 marchers including 3,000 white sympathizers gathered in front of the Lincoln Memorial in Washington, D. C. Starting at noon until three o'clock, a number of important black leaders addressed the crowd. When Martin was introduced and made the closing address, Coretta sat beside the radio at home listening to Martin's words in rapt attention. She missed being there but she was proud of her husband's inspiring speech, the first one he had ever made to a national audience. Calling for a strong leadership from the federal government, from white liberals, from the white moderates of the South, and for courageous leadership from the black community, Martin ended with a rousing appeal to "give us the ballot and we will write the proper laws on the books."

From 1957 to 1958 Martin delivered over 200 speeches and traveled over 750,000 miles. The young black leader was in great demand, receiving invitations from all over the world, and though Coretta missed him, she never questioned why he had to go. Despite his many commitments, Martin also managed to write his first book, *Stride Toward Freedom.* Because of constant interruptions, sometimes he had to hide out in the homes of friends so that he could complete the manuscript.

On October 23, 1957, Martin came home for the birth of his first son, Martin Luther King, Jr. III. Coretta did not believe it was a good idea to name the child after his father. She felt it might be a problem in the future to have the same name as a famous parent, but it meant so much to Martin that she finally went along with it.

When the baby was nearly a year old, Coretta and Martin took their first real vacation since their marriage. Leaving official business and speeches behind, they spent two weeks in Mexico trying to relax. They enjoyed the beauty of the countryside but, even though they were on vacation, the great differences they observed between the rich and the poor were very disturbing to them. To recognize and fight poverty and justice wherever it existed had become a way of life for Coretta and Martin.

Soon after they returned home, the Kings were plunged into one crisis after the other. The first one occurred on September 3, 1958. Coretta and Martin had accompanied Ralph Abernathy to the courthouse in Montgomery where Ralph was to testify in a private case. As they stood in a group outside the courtroom, a policeman ordered them to move on. Martin tried to explain that they were waiting for a lawyer. The officer, however, insulted him, calling him "boy" and ordering him to move again. When Martin refused, he was pushed, roughed up, and arrested for "loitering." Bewildered and upset, Coretta ran to get help. When she returned, she found that on discovering who Martin was, he had been charged with disobeying an officer and released. A trial was set for a few days later, but Martin knew he would be convicted and fined. He told Coretta, "The time has come when I should no longer accept bail. If I commit a crime in the name of civil rights, I will go to jail and serve the time."

Coretta agreed with her husband that the time had come for someone to take the risk and that he was the best person to do it. She knew that Martin was certainly not anxious to go to jail, but she also agreed that it would arouse sympathy for the civil rights movement if he were imprisoned. At this time Martin was responding to the influence of Mahatma Ghandi and his method of peaceful non cooperation. He felt that black leadership must be prepared to make sacrifices for their people just as Ghandi had made sacrifices for his people.

When Martin's trial came up, he was found guilty and sentenced to a fine of $10 or fourteen days in jail. The judge was surprised when Martin refused to pay the fine. As Martin tried to enter the prison van with the other prisoners, he was stopped by the guards. Finally he was told that he was free to go because someone had paid his fine. Since Martin had told his friends of his plans and asked them not to pay his fine, he insisted on knowing who had paid it. When he persisted, he was informed that the person wished to remain anonymous. Martin learned later that the anonymous person was the police commissioner, Clyde Sellers. Mr. Sellers had paid the fine out of his own pocket because he didn't want to give Dr. King any more publicity.

Martin's first book was published in September 1958. *Stride Toward Freedom*, the story of the Montgomery bus boycott, received excellent reviews and the author departed on a lecture tour around the country to introduce his book to the public. Crowds turned out to see him in all the major cities, but one of the largest turnouts was in New York City, in the black neighborhood of Harlem.

In the shoe department of Blumstein's Department store, Martin sat at a table autographing books when a middle-aged black woman approached him. Staring intently at the man at the table, she asked, "Are you Dr. King?" When the author asserted that he was, the woman leaned across the table and plunged a steel letter opener into Martin's chest.

That night Coretta had expected a phone call from her husband asking her to pick him up at the airport. Instead she received a call informing her that Martin had been stabbed by a mentally disturbed woman and was in the Harlem Hospital. As she prepared to fly to New York, Coretta alternately sobbed and prayed that the terrible nightmares she recently had about Martin getting killed would not come true. At the hospital, the chief surgeon and the three man team who had operated on Martin told her how close to death he had come. The edge of the knife had been so near his heart that a sudden movement would have caused instant death. The surgeon felt that Dr. King's wonderful attitude and cooperation had helped to save his life. "As you well know," said Dr. Maynard, "your husband is an extraordinary man."

Of course no one knew that better than Coretta Scott King. She thanked God for the miracle of Martin's life but she could not help feeling that the ordeal they had lived through was "preparing them for something that was still to come."

Martin had often spoken "of violence and being able to accept a blow without striking back." Now both of them felt that those words were being put to the test. As soon as Martin could speak, he urged that Isola Curry, the woman who had attacked him, should not be prosecuted, but instead helped to heal from her mental affliction because he felt she was not responsible for her act. Some time later, Mrs. Curry was committed to an institution for the criminally insane.

On October 25th, Coretta took Martin's place at an important event. In Washington, D. C. at the youth March for Integrated Schools, Mrs. King, along with singer Harry Belafonte, baseball star Jackie Robinson, and A. Philip Randolph, head of the Brotherhood of Sleeping Car Porters, a black labor union, led the march. As 10,000 people consisting mostly of college students, gave her all their attention, Coretta delivered the speech Martin had prepared. The ability to remain calm under pressure was no longer a new experience for the young woman. Living through times of tension and crisis had taught her to be stronger and more poised than she ever thought possible. Coretta Scott King was now Martin Luther King Jr's partner and co-worker in the fullest and most important sense of both words.

Chapter VII
MOUNTAINS TO CLIMB

It took Martin a while to recover from his ordeal, but when he felt better he thought it might be the right time to accept an invitation to visit India. For a long time he had wanted to see for himself the country set free by Mahatma Gandhi, its leaders, and talk with the people who had worked with him. He was also interested in seeing why the Montgomery bus boycotts had been compared to Gandhi's protest marches against British rule. Almost a year ago Martin had been asked by the Gandhi Peace Foundation to make a speaking tour of India, but the Kings could not afford either the time or money to make the trip. In March, 1959, when the Christopher Reynolds Foundation offered them a grant of $5,000, Martin and Coretta flew to India.

Their first sight of India was a bit of a shock. When the plane circled over the city of Bombay, they looked down on a brightly-lit harbor bustling with activity. However, once they landed, they were driven through filthy, winding streets crowded with people wearing rags, sleeping on the streets and in doorways. Coretta realized these were homeless people and that the bundles of newspapers under their heads carried everything they owned. The sight of half-naked, skeleton-like human beings crouching over garbage cans in search of food was terribly upsetting to Coretta and Martin. Even in Africa they had never seen such abject poverty. It was hard for the American visitors to understand or accept these deplorable conditions.

Before they left the United States, the Kings had been warned against giving money to beggars because the government wanted to discourage this practice. Nevertheless when an emaciated man with a baby in his arms approached them and pointed to his mouth, then the child's mouth to show they were starving, Martin and Coretta poured all their change into the beggar's outstretched hand.

The next day they flew to New Delhi where they were invited to dinner at the home of Prime Minister Jawaharlah Nehru. After so much poverty, the luxurious surrounding of the official residence came as a sharp contrast. For the next few hours the two leaders talked about Gandhi's philosophy of non-violence, and Nehru commended Martin for following a similar philosophy in the struggle for civil rights in America. Coretta did a lot of listening, but later on she felt, "I would have talked about the women of India had I realized how much progress they had made with the coming of Independence." Gandhi had involved the women of India in the struggle for freedom and some of them had even gone to jail along with the men. Coretta promised herself she would increase her activities in women's organizations that addressed vital issues once she returned to the United States.

During their stay in India, Coretta and Martin continued to observe contrasting lifestyles among the people. Those who were Gandhi's followers dressed and lived very simply while others lived in elegant homes built by the British and copied Western civilizations. As they traveled, Martin gave talks to the Indian people, telling them how much he was influenced by Gandhi's principles. On many of these programs, Coretta sang Negro spirituals and was happy to find her songs warmly received by Indian audiences who had never heard spirituals before.

Despite the vast differences between the rich and the poor, the Indian experience made a great impression on Martin's thinking. He tried to visualize how the ideals of simple living could be applied to daily life in America. He even considered changing his own style of dress but then he realized that this might turn off people because they might not understand it. Martin confessed to Coretta that his conscience troubled him because he was not giving up things like a car and a comfortable home to set a good example to others. Finally the black leader's common sense told him that he could not accomplish the things he wanted unless hc had a car in which to travel and a home where he could stay. It took some time to arrive at the decision that the best he could do was to accept the conditions of his American lifestyle but strive to be more like Gandhi in spiritual matters.

Though his growing family could have used a bigger home and car, Martin chose to give most of his speaking fees to the civil rights movement to pay its salaries, rents, and other expenses. Many black people felt "that nothing was too good for Dr. King, that he should ride in Cadillacs behind motor cycles," because, "they like to think of him as the President of the Negroes." Though Martin was deeply devoted to the Movement, the idea was not at all in keeping with his feelings about himself. He did not want to be thought of as better than any other man and continued to live as modestly as possible.

Toward the end of 1959, Martin made an important decision. In order to give more time to the civil rights struggle, he felt he could no longer continue in the position of full-time pastor at the Dexter Avenue Baptist Church. In Atlanta, Georgia, the Ebenezer Baptist Church, where Martin's father had been a pastor for many years, offered the young man a position as co-pastor. Though the salary was only $4,200 a year, it would leave him the time needed to devote to the SCLC and other important projects for the movement. When necessary he would supplement the family income from part of his speaking fees.

Now that the bus boycott was over, Coretta and Martin knew there would be other "mountains" to climb, but they were prepared to scale them together. Leaving Montgomery and their first church was a wrenching experience because the Kings had grown close to the congregation. The congregation members were equally sad about losing their beloved pastor and his wife.

On the last Sunday in January, 1960, a farewell ceremony in the couple's honor took place in the Dexter Avenue Baptist Church. After the service the congregation presented the Kings with a beautiful silver tea set. Then everyone rose and sang "Blest Be The Tie That Binds." Coretta and Martin made no attempt to hide their tears. They left Montgomery knowing that the six years they had spent there were a very important and meaningful part of their lives. Not only had they made many friends and followers, they had helped to lay the foundation for the Civil Rights Movement and its future.

Shortly after the Kings moved to Atlanta, Martin suffered a serious attack on his reputation. He was indicted on a charge of falsifying his Alabama State income tax returns. The implication was that he had received money from the MIA and SCLC and not reported it. Since Martin was very careful and thorough keeping accounts and Coretta was extremely organized, they were shocked and upset by the unfounded charges. Though his family and friends all tried to reassure Martin, the attack on his personal honesty was the most hurtful thing that had ever happened to him. It was troubling to think that people who didn't know him might believe the false charge; but as usual, the community stood by him and contributed to his defense. In Montgomery, on Saturday, May 28th, the case went before a jury of twelve white men. Coretta was hopeful that justice would prevail, but she could not help feeling nervous all the same. When the foreman of the jury pronounced the words "Not guilty", Martin's wife was overcome with relief and happiness.

That same evening Coretta was scheduled to speak in Cleveland, Ohio, for the Antioch Baptist Church Women's Day. Because there had not been time to write a speech, she could not decide about what to talk. Finally she made up her mind to speak extemporaneously about her recent experience in court, the endless hours of waiting, the anxiety, and the joyous conclusion. No sooner was Coretta introduced to the audience, then the words came tumbling out while the people listened spellbound for forty minutes. All Coretta felt was "thankful that the spirit had guided me on this occasion."

With each successful experience in public speaking, Coretta grew increasingly more confident about addressing large audiences. She also started to develop interests outside the home which proved to be very rewarding. Through her concerts and speeches, she was able to contribute to the cause for civil rights, and when she moved to Atlanta, she became a member of the Women's International League for Peace and Freedom.

In 1957 the National Council of Negro Women presented Coretta with their annual Brotherhood Award.

By 1960, boycotts and protests had become an
important part of life in the South. Among the frustrating aspects of segregation for black people was the
situation which prevented them from being served in
restaurants and at lunch counters. At that time there
were still signs posted in eating places that read, "For
Colored Only."

On February 1, 1960, in the town of Greensboro,
North Carolina, three black college students attempted
to sit down at a lunch counter in a Woolworth Store and
wait to be served. The students were well-dressed and
spoke in a courteous manner, but when they ordered
coffee, the waitress refused to serve them because they
were black. The students continued to sit quietly,
refusing to leave. The next day, and the day after that,
they returned and were joined by both white and black
students from the University of North Carolina and
Bennett College. In a few day, the newspapers circulated
the story throughout the South. Soon more and more
protests called "sit-ins" continued to be conducted by
college students wherever there were lunch counters.

At some of the sit-ins, young people carried signs
that read, "Remember the teachings of Gandhi and
Martin Luther King, Jr." When Martin learned about
this, he was very impressed and touched that students
wanted to take on the serious responsibility of protest-
ing. He was also concerned that violence against them
would erupt and that they would be arrested, a situation
which soon came to pass. However, when students were
attacked or arrested, the next day, more students came
to take their place. Though Martin realized that brave
young people like these could be a strong force in the

movement, he was also aware of the need for organization. After holding a meeting with other black leaders, a new civil rights group was formed called the Student Nonviolent Coordinating Committee (SNCC).

Though a number of the older members of the SNCC did not approve of the actions of the young protesters, Martin believed in the college students and joined some of their sit-ins. As a result, the black leader was put in jail several times.

At this time Yoki was nearly five years old and Marty was nearly three. One afternoon the children heard the news on the radio that their father had been arrested. It was the first time they were aware of what was happening and they were very upset. Yoki started to cry.

"Why does Daddy have to go to jail?" she asked Coretta.

For some time, Coretta had been trying to prepare herself to explain the situation to the children but now she knew it could not wait. She wanted to give them an answer they could understand, but one that was honest, too. Finally she said, "Your daddy is a brave and kind man. He went to jail to help people. Some people don't have enough to eat or comfortable homes in which to live, or enough clothing to wear. Daddy went to jail to make it possible for all people to have these things. Don't worry, your daddy will be coming back."

These words helped to reassure the children. When a little white girl in Yoki's class said to her, "Your daddy is always going to jail," Yoki was able to answer quite calmly, "Yes, he goes to jail to help people." The pride in her voice was so obvious that her classmate never brought the subject up again.

Each time that Martin went to jail, Coretta felt that a part of her was imprisoned with him. She very much wanted to share this experience, but Martin made her realize that the children were too young for both their parents to be away from them at the same time. Right now Coretta was also pregnant with their third child.

A shocking incident occurred when Martin was arrested for driving with an expired license and sentenced to six months in jail at hard labor. Back in April or May of 1960, Martin had neglected to change his Alabama driving license for one from Georgia. A charge of this kind usually did not result in being jailed, but Martin had the reputation of being a black man who stirred up "trouble" for white people in the South. To spend six months in prison for a traffic violation was a harsh and unjust sentence. When Coretta heard the verdict, she could not help breaking down in tears. She not only felt bad for Martin, but the thought that such a long sentence meant her husband would be in jail while their baby was being born, was almost too much to bear.

She tried to visit him every day but soon the daily trips made her feel strained and exhausted.

What happened next came as still another shock. Without any warning, in the middle of the night, Martin was handcuffed, put in chains and driven to another prison three hundred miles away where he was thrown into a solitary cell. Coretta had told their children their father had to go to jail to help people, but this was different. She felt frightened and frustrated, but Daddy King told her they would get lawyers to help have Martin released from prison as soon as they could. While they were preparing to meet with the lawyers, suddenly the phone rang.

The voice at the other end said that Senator John Kennedy wanted to speak with Mrs. King. At this time Senator Kennedy was running for the office of president of the United States. When he learned of the serious injustice against Dr. King, he was very concerned and asked Coretta how he could help. Coretta replied that she would appreciate anything he could do for her husband.

Of course it was exciting to know that a well-known Senator was interested in Martin's case, but Coretta didn't know if this would change the situation. Much to her great joy and gratitude, Martin was released and came home the next day.

On November 8, 1960, John F. Kennedy was elected President of the United States. It was believed by some people that the extra votes needed to achieve the election had been won because of the candidate's intervention in Martin's predicament.

On January 30, 1961, Coretta gave birth to a baby boy. The Kings named him Dexter after the church in which Martin had preached. As the months passed, many successful sit-ins took place in areas around the South. Members of the SNCC also organized a protest against segregated interstate buses. Just as they had ignored the segregated signs at lunch counters, protesters climbed on interstate buses and sat anywhere there were empty seats. The trips were called *Freedom Rides*, but many of them were far from peaceful. Southern whites showed their opposition by acts of violence every day, attacking buses with rocks, guns, and bombs but the black riders refused to react with similar acts of violence. Some white people who were sympathetic to the civil rights cause helped by joining the Freedom Riders. Though Martin spoke to many Freedom Riders, he did not have the time to ride with them and some of the students were upset about this. As for Coretta, she was busy caring for the new baby and could only watch events on television. She was miserable about her husband's abscncc, but she knew it was the price she had to pay as the wife of a great leader. Nevertheless, Coretta continued to organize things behind the scenes, giving concerts and speeches to gain moral and financial support whenever and wherever possible.

In March 1962, Coretta received an exciting invitation from a women's group called the Women's Strike For Peace. By now many people knew that Mrs. King was actively interested in promoting world peace. World leaders were planning to meet in Geneva, Switzerland, to discuss banning the testing of atomic weapons, and the Women's Strike For Peace group planned to represent their individual countries, contributing their insights on how atomic tests would affect average citizens.

Martin encouraged Coretta to attend the conference but she didn't know how she could manage it. To start with, she was supposed to give a concert in Cincinnati on the Sunday night the group planned to return. There was also the problem of arranging for a responsible baby sitter for a whole week. Finally, somehow, it all worked out. Coretta was able to join fifty American women on the trip to Geneva. There were four black women in the group, and Coretta was proud to be one of them. In Geneva they were joined by women from England, Australia, Russia, Scandinavia and other countries, but Americans comprised the majority. Every woman was concerned with stopping all wars, but especially in achieving a nuclear test ban treaty. Though no major change resulted from the convention, Coretta was very impressed with the women she met. She returned home, more committed to peace than ever.

On March 28, 1963, the King's fourth child, Bernice Albertine, was born. She was nicknamed *Bunny* and though her father was there to welcome her, he had to leave for Alabama the next day. Because of all the protest marches, Coretta knew Martin would be arrested again. She had looked forward to having her husband spend Easter with the family, but it did not happen. When she did not hear from Martin, she realized he must be in jail. The first thing he always did after being arrested was to call her. This time there was no call.

Over the weekend Coretta waited anxiously for the phone to ring. When it didn't, she became upset and worried for Martin's safety. Suddenly John Kennedy's words about helping her if she needed it came back to her. She didn't want Martin released from prison because that would have defeated their purpose. All she wanted was to hear her husband's voice and be able to talk to him. Acting on impulse, she called the White House number that President Kennedy had given her but he was not in Washington. All Coretta could do was leave a message with the president's press secretary, Pierre Salinger, who promised to give the president her message as soon as he returned.

As Coretta sat waiting, the phone rang again. To her surprise, this call was from the president's brother, Robert Kennedy who was the United States Attorney General. He listened to Coretta and then told her he would reach the president as soon as possible. On Monday afternoon, there was one more call. It was President Kennedy.

The president explained that he had been with his father who was ill, but that he was very concerned about

Martin's situation. He also told her that the FBI had gone to Birmingham to check on Martin and that he was all right. Fifteen minutes later Martin called and reassured Coretta that not only was he all right, but that he was suddenly receiving much better treatment at the prison than he had at first.

Martin was in prison for eight days. While he was there, several local white ministers put an ad in the paper saying that Martin was a troublemaker. Feeling it was necessary to respond, Martin wrote a letter to the ministers and the world, explaining why protests against racism could not wait. Called "Letter from a Birmingham Jail" it was published in newspapers throughout the country and became one of the most famous documents of the civil rights movement.

On April 20th, Martin was finally released. The letter he had written made him and the Movement nationally known and respected by those who believed in justice and equality for human beings everywhere.

Chapter VIII
DEATH OF A LEADER

In 1963, the city of Birmingham, Alabama, had the reputation for being the "most segregated city in the South." The governor, George Wallace, believed that white people were superior to black people and that segregation should continue as a perfectly normal way of life in the South. Black leaders realized that demonstrators were needed to protest but many of the black adults in Birmingham were worried that if they protested there would be retaliation from the white community and the loss of their jobs. For the first time it was decided that black school children should be allowed to march in the protests.

The leaders felt that Birmingham's school children would make excellent demonstrators for two reasons. One was that the children did not have to fear losing employment. The other was that when the newspapers published pictures of youngsters being arrested and thrown in jail, the whole country would see what Birmingham authorities were really like.

On May 2, 1963, the Children's Crusade in Birmingham began. Children too young to march pleaded to join but only those between the ages of six and eighteen were accepted. Those who were selected were carefully instructed by teachers and parents how to act. Marching slowly side by side the children sang, "We Shall Overcome." But before long, the police moved in to arrest them. No sooner did this happen then more children replaced them, continuing to march and sing. That day, 959 young people were arrested.

The next day when more young marchers arrived, the Commissioner of Public Safety, Eugene "Bull" Connor ordered the city's police dogs to attack, while firemen opened fire hoses and knocked the children down by showering them with powerful jets of water.

As people around the country witnessed the terrible scenes on TV, they grew shocked and furious. For the next four days, as children continued to be attacked by snarling dogs and streams of water, news photographers took photos and reported the events around the world. Soon, letters and telegrams came pouring into the White House. President Kennedy responded by going on TV appealing to all Americans to eliminate segregation. He stated that he planned to ask Congress to pass laws that would grant equal rights to all races.

On June 19, 1963, President Kennedy kept his promise by delivering a civil rights bill to Congress for passage. However, Martin and other black leaders could not be sure that the bill would be passed. Coretta told Martin she thought this might be the right time for a March on Washington. "I believe a hundred thousand people would come to the nation's capital at your invitation."

At a conference with many black leaders the idea of a peaceful demonstration to put pressure on the passage of the Civil Rights Bill was positively received. A number of white leaders joined the effort to appeal to Congress and the march was scheduled for August 28, 1963. Coretta was anxious to be among those leading the march but it was decided by the planning council that the march should be led by only the top men. Coretta felt that she belonged by Martin's side on this special day but she had no choice. Nevertheless, she marched behind her husband along with the Abernathys, Dr. Ralph Bunche, former ambassador to the United Nations, Lena Horne, and many other famous people who believed in the Movement. She was lucky to obtain a seat directly behind Martin on the speaker's platform where she could see and hear everything. When Martin was introduced, Coretta was thrilled at the tremendous reception given to him by the largest crowd she had ever seen.

Though he had prepared a written speech, Martin was so moved that he started speaking from the heart. As he came to the words, "Freedom Now", and "Jobs Now", they rang in a rhythmic beat which was picked up by the crowd as they shouted "Now" together with him. While 250,000 people of different races and religions lifted their faces toward him, Martin told them about his "Dream." In impassioned language that has since been quoted countless times over the years, he told the multitude about his dream of a nation where his four children would be judged by the content of their character, not the color of their skin.

With his resonant voice soaring above the crowd, Martin poured out his heart. "When all God's children, black men and white men, Jews and Gentiles, Protestants and Catholics will be able to join hands and sing -- Free at last!"

As he ended his speech, there was a moment of awed silence. Then 250,000 people rose to their feet and shouted and cheered until they were hoarse. Surrounded by United States marshals trying to protect him from the surging crowds, Coretta barely managed to get to her husband to tell him how proud she was before he was whisked into a car that took him to the White House for a conference with the president.

Though the march on Washington was the highlight of the year for Coretta, it was followed by several tragic episodes.

On September 15, 1963, a black church was bombed in Birmingham and four little girls were killed. It happened on a Sunday morning while the children were in Sunday School. Coretta and Martin visited the families of Cynthia Wesley, Carole Robertson, Addie Mae Collins, and Denise McNair. Martin also preached at the girls' funerals.

Two months later, on November 22, 1963, another shocking tragedy occurred. While Martin was watching TV he saw a news bulletin flash on the screen announcing that President Kennedy had been shot down in Dallas. When Martin interrupted Coretta who was talking on the phone to tell her the news, she hung up and sat beside him, holding his hand. Together they prayed that John Kennedy would not die. They knew it would not only be a real national disaster, but that his death would also affect the Movement. The president had been a strong believer in civil rights and with him at the head of the American government, the Cause would have an opportunity to make progress in the future. When the announcement came through that the President was dead, Martin grew very pale. Turning to Coretta, he said, "This is what is going to happen to me also." Coretta could find no words to comfort her husband because in her heart she felt he was probably right. All she could do was sit close beside him and hold his hand. Coretta was as deeply affected by the President's untimely death as she had been by Martin's stabbing in Harlem. She realized that Martin's work was much more dangerous than the president's had been. As she watched the somber funeral scenes on TV, Coretta had the strange feeling she would be seeing them again in the near future.

Shortly after Vice President Lyndon Johnson became president of the United States, he urged Congress to pass the Civil Rights Act in memory of John Kennedy. On July 22, 1964, Martin was invited to the White House for the signing of the bill which outlawed segregated public facilities in the United States.

Another exciting event occurred when Martin was notified he had been awarded the Nobel Peace Prize for 1964. This prize is the highest award in the world given to the individual who had made the most outstanding contribution to peace that year. At the age of thirty five, Martin was one of the youngest people ever to receive the Nobel Peace Prize. On December 4, 1964, Coretta, Martin, their parents and some of their friends, including the Abernathys, flew to London. At St. Paul's Cathedral, Martin was invited to preach a sermon. From there the King party went on to Oslo, Norway, where Martin was presented with the prize of $54,000 at Oslo University.

Coretta thought that part of the prize money should be used for their children's education, but Martin wanted to use the money only for the cause of civil rights. Coretta finally had to agree that support for the Movement was an important priority. She was very proud of her husband and tried to go along with his ideas as much as possible. She also knew that there were more struggles ahead because before they left there had been rumors that the F.B.I. (Federal Bureau of Investigation) was looking to discredit Martin Luther King, Jr.

When a grand ball was given by African students from Kenya in the King's honor in the city of Stockholm, Sweden, the young people insisted that Coretta and Martin dance the first dance. Baptist ministers and their wives rarely had an opportunity to dance. Coretta really enjoyed this experience but the next day they had to fly home to face the problems that were waiting for them.

Soon after their return, Coretta received a tape in the mail along with a threatening letter addressed to Dr. King. The tape was not very clear, but Martin's voice and the voice of an unidentified woman were recognizable. Realizing that the FBI was trying to undermine her husband's reputation, Coretta refused to let their ugly scare tactics disturb her relationship with Martin. She passed the tapes on to the SCLC and went on with the more important aspects of her life.

Though more people, both black and white, were working for the Movement, 1964 was one of the worst years as far as violence was concerned. On Sunday, June 21, 1964, Coretta and Martin received the shocking news that three young volunteer civil rights workers -- one black and two white -- had been arrested in Mississippi. Michael Schwerner, James Chaney, and Andrew Goodman had come South to join the Movement. After being arrested on speeding charges, the young men had disappeared. Local authorities claimed they had been released from jail a few hours after their arrest. Their burned out station wagon was discovered a few days later, but it was not until August 4th, that their bodies were found buried in an earthen dam.

Martin delivered the memorial service for the slain civil rights workers, and a fund was established called the Goodman-Chaney-Schwerner Fund. In order to raise money for this fund as well as the SCLC Coretta started giving Freedom Concerts again. She used the same format that had been successful in New York in 1956 and was able to raise more than $50,000.

In the Spring of 1965, Martin and members of the SCLC made plans to move into Alabama to help black citizens demonstrate for voter registration. Up until that time black people who wished to register to vote would have to stand in line all day waiting for the registration office to open. At the end of the day a clerk would come out and tell those on line that the office was closed, even though it had never opened. Sometimes the door would open to admit one or two black people out of a hundred to register while the others were turned away. This unjust procedure continued until March 5, 1965, when Martin urged President Johnson to pass the Voting Rights Bill. Such a bill would guarantee all Americans the right to vote no matter to which race they belonged.

In order to draw attention to the problem, Martin and other black leaders organized a protest march from Selma, Alabama, to the state capitol fifty miles away in Montgomery. Governor Wallace immediately issued an order forbidding the march, but the plans for a peaceful demonstration continued.

On Sunday, March 7, 1965, one of the most vicious attacks on nonviolent protesters in history took place. As 1500 marchers tried to cross the Pettus Bridge in Selma, state troopers warned them they had three minutes to stop and go back. Some of the protesters did stop, but they did not turn back. Instead they got down on their knees and started to pray. Mounted on horses, and wearing gas masks, the troopers charged into the kneeling men and women, attacking them with clubs, whips, electric cattle prods and tear gas.

While seventy or eighty marchers were injured and taken to the hospital, TV cameras recorded the shocking scene for viewers around the country. One result was that hundreds of volunteers starting arriving in Alabama to join in the protests. Another was the marchers went to court to obtain an order preventing the march from being stopped. Following SCLC policy, Martin did not lead the march because the leadership wanted Dr. King to be available to meet with President Johnson.

On March 15, 1965, the President urged Congress to pass a new bill insuring voting rights for all people. He concluded his speech with the words that became the rallying cry of black people around the country, "We shall overcome." A few days later a federal court ruled that the Selma to Montgomery march was legal.

Leading 3,200 protesters, on Sunday, March 21st, Martin Luther King Jr. and Ralph Abernathy marched across the Pettus Bridge. Among the marchers were white clergymen and nuns from the North as well as famous entertainers and politicians, both white and black. Because Coretta had a commitment to speak in North Carolina that day she was unable to be in on the start of the march. However, on Monday Coretta joined the march, walking alongside of Martin and Rosa Parks on Highway 80 toward Montgomery. The next few days seemed endless but on Thursday, the final day of the march, thousands of volunteers arrived by bus, car, train, and plane, joining the others for the last two miles of the journey. This time there were no attacks, and by the end of the march, 25,000 people had taken part in the victorious demonstration.

On August 6, 1965, the Voting Rights Act was signed into law by President Johnson. This was an important step toward equality for black people. Now black voters across the South were able to cast their votes in voting polls like all Americans. Though she was thrilled at what the march had accomplished, Coretta was aware that African Americans still had other challenges to face in their struggle for equality.

In 1966, black leaders decided it was time to address the issue of poverty and other economic problems in northern and western cities across the country. Up until this time, protests for civil rights had been focused mostly in the South. Though black people in northern cities could vote and did not ride in segregated buses, they suffered from other inequities and discrimination.

In January, the city of Chicago, Illinois was selected as a target spot for the SCLC drive in order to draw attention to the problems in the black ghetto. Because Coretta and Martin wanted to learn firsthand about the conditions they were trying to improve, they rented an apartment in a slum neighborhood and lived there with their children. When the landlord learned that Dr. King and his family would be his tenants, he did his best to fix up the apartment, but Coretta was shocked when she first saw it.

The apartment was on the third floor. The flights of stairs leading up to it were broken and shaky, and there were no lights in the hall. There was barely any heat and the kitchen had an old refrigerator that did not work. The owner had made an attempt to paint the rooms, but the old paint underneath had swelled and the result was bulging, smeared-looking walls. The worst part was the overpowering smell of urine in the halls where drunk people had come in off the street to use the place as a toilet. It was hard to believe that the rent for the King's apartment was $90 a month.

Coretta tried to make their living quarters as presentable as possible but second hand furniture, curtains, and plants did not really change the basic conditions. Though the King children had lived pretty simply at home they had never experienced real poverty. Without trees or grass, they played in the street like the other kids, surrounded by traffic, dirt, and noise. Before long, Coretta was aware that her children were behaving differently, fighting and screaming at each other until she had to make them stop. It was hurtful to realize this was the everyday way of life for children who lived there with no hope of anything better.

Martin hoped he could improve some of the conditions in the slums of Chicago. The Kings and members of the SCLC staff cleaned the building where they lived and moved out piles of garbage. Martin met with the tenants and encouraged them not to pay rent but to use the money to fix up the building on their own. He also met with street gangs in the neighborhood, held rallies and planned a march to city hall.

As the news got around that Dr. King was a neighbor, people sought him out to talk about their problems. Martin and Coretta spoke with teenage gang members, trying to impress them with the importance of nonviolent tactics. Some of the teenagers listened and joined the Movement. However, Chicago was a big city and Martin could not reach every African American the way he would have liked.

A protest rally on July 10, 1966, was followed the next evening by a riot. The day after Coretta had been scheduled to speak to a women's group at the YWCA on the topic of unity. Because of the violent turn of events she decided not to give a speech. Instead she asked the audience to join her in sending a telegram of protest to the mayor of Chicago urging him to make the city a better place in which to live. The same afternoon Coretta and the women's group formed an organization called Women Mobilized for Change. In a short time it attracted more than 1,000 members in the Chicago area.

After receiving the telegram, Mayor Richard Daley promised to clean up the slums and develop a policy for open housing and better job opportunities for black citizens. As the summer passed and nothing was done, other riots broke out around the city.

The King children were due back in school and Coretta took them home to Atlanta. Despite some negative aspects, she felt it had been important to expose them to the reality of life in the ghetto. Martin stayed on to organize more marches and try to meet with Mayor Daley. At a conference with the mayor, representatives of the Chicago Housing Authority and black leaders in Chicago, an agreement on open housing was finally reached.

Another project called Operation Breadbasket was organized by the SCLC and led by the Reverend Jesse Jackson. In October, 1967, Coretta attended one of Rev. Jackson's meetings and was very impressed with the feeling of unity with which the audience responded to the speaker. She came home and told Martin, "I think that Jesse Jackson and Operation Breadbasket have something that is needed in every community." In the months that followed, under Jackson's guidance, housing and employment conditions gradually improved for black people in Chicago.

In 1967 as the United States became involved in the war in Vietnam, Martin began to speak out against the evils of war. Vietnam was a small nation in Asia that had been fighting a civil war for many years. In the

1960's when the conflict first got under way, only a few United States advisors were sent to help the Vietnamese government oppose the communist rebels. Then when China and Russia sent aid to the communists in North Vietnam, the United States sent equipment and men to support the people of South Vietnam. Soon thousands of young American soldiers, many of them African Americans, were fighting and losing their lives in the war in Vietnam.

Coretta felt the same way about the war that her husband did. She joined Martin in speaking at peace demonstrations. They both urged the government to end its involvement in Vietnam. Some leaders, however, disagreed with Martin and Coretta. They believed that the King's statements against the war could hurt the civil rights movement. They felt that all Martin's efforts should go towards helping his own people. As for Coretta, the more her husband was criticized, the more she defended him. She believed that Martin's participation in the drive to end the Vietnam War was a turning point for the peace movement and for the nation. She also felt it would be hypocritical for a minister to speak out against the evils of society and not the evils of war. She pointed out that Pope Paul VI had spoken out against war, and wondered why a black man who was also a clergyman could not do the same thing without being criticized.

During 1967 Martin and his family lived under constantly growing tension. There were more riots than ever before which greatly distressed the black leader. Some people said the nonviolent movement had failed, but Coretta did her best to encourage Martin. "There are millions of people who have faith in you and feel that you are our best hope." Then she added, "I believe in you, if that means anything." And Martin replied, "Yes, it means a great deal."

In January 1967, Martin went to Jamaica in the Caribbean Islands to write his fourth book, "Where Do We Go From Here? Chaos or Community." Though he wrote twelve to fifteen hours a day, when Coretta joined him for a week they enjoyed a lovely vacation. Martin also dedicated the book to Coretta. During this time the couple had more quality communication than they had in a long time. Sometimes Martin seemed depressed, and though he was not morbid about the subject of death, both he and Coretta had a premonition that something bad threatened their lives. There had been several death threats but they tried not to brood about them.

In February Martin delivered a sermon at the Ebenzer Baptist Church which reflected his anxiety. "If any of you are around when I have to meet my day," he told the congregation, "I don't want a long funeral." As he continued Martin spoke of reaching a mountain top in his life and that he was not afraid. As he concluded by quoting from "The Battle Hymn of the Republic" -- "Mine eyes have seen the glory of the coming of the Lord," the audience shouted out its approval and love and the black leader was overcome with emotion.

In March 1968, Martin learned about a series of nonviolent protests conducted by the black sanitation workers of Memphis, Tennessee. The employees were striking for better wages and working conditions, and Martin decided to travel to Memphis to lend his support. He made several trips to investigate the problems caused by the conflict between the peaceful protesters and the more aggressive demonstrators. On April 3rd Martin left for what was to be his last plane trip. Because it was a 7:00 A.M. flight, the children were still asleep, but Coretta followed Martin to the door and kissed him good-bye.

Due to a bomb threat the plane's arrival was delayed, but Martin managed to stay in good spirits. He and Ralph Abernathy were busy planning to lead a protest demonstration with the sanitation workers. Martin and his staff arrived in Memphis on Thursday night, April 4, 1968 and checked into the Lorraine Motel. Before they went down to dinner Martin and the others came out to relax on the motel balcony outside Ralph's room. The night air was pleasant and they stood there talking and laughing. Then Ralph said he had forgotten to put on some shaving lotion and went back inside.

Suddenly a shot rang out and a bullet wounded Martin Luther King Jr. in the neck. The black leader crumpled to the ground and lay there motionless. Jesse Jackson, the young minister who had come to Memphis to work with Dr. King, rushed to call Coretta. He told her that her husband had been shot and was in the hospital.

Acting quickly, Coretta arranged for a baby sitter to stay with the children, reserved a seat on the next flight out and drove to the airport. While she waited to board the plane, she heard her name being paged. Suddenly an icy shiver ran down Coretta's spine. Before she heard the words, she knew the news had to be bad. Then the words came out, and they were like the tolling of a spectral bell.

"Mrs. King, I have been asked to tell you -- Dr. King is dead."

Chapter IX
ON WITH THE DREAM

In the days that followed, Coretta had to call on every bit of inner strength and courage in order to cope with the nightmare that confronted her. Despite the outpouring of sympathy that came from family, friends and well-wishers around the world, she needed to find some kind of meaning in her husband's tragic death.

One thought that provided some consolation was the realization that Martin's death had happened close to the anniversary of the death of Jesus. She remembered that Martin had frequently talked about the meaning of Easter. He believed that moments of despair were the Good Fridays of life, but even in the darkest moments something was bound to happen, and then there would be light and hope once more.

Explaining to the children about their father was a heart-breaking situation. When the youngest child, Bunny, asked, "Where's Daddy?" all Coretta could answer was, "Daddy has gone to live with God, and he won't be coming back." When twelve year old Yoki, tears running down her cheeks, asked, "Should I hate the man who killed my daddy?" Coretta answered, "No, darling, your daddy wouldn't want you to do that."

Through all the pain and anguish felt by Coretta she tried to make certain that her children would not hate or become bitter because that was what Martin would have wanted. In his lifetime, despite the most harrowing experiences, he had encouraged his family not to hate, and now Coretta strove to carry out his teaching.

On Sunday, April 6, President Johnson declared a national day of mourning. The day before Coretta appeared at Ebenezer Baptist Church to make a public statement to the congregation. She told them that Martin had been prepared to give his life for what he believed, and that her religious faith was giving her the strength to bear her burdens. Many people admired Coretta King and respected her message, but there were others who did not. Angry and bitter over the black leader's assassination, these individuals participated in riots in more than a hundred cities around the country.

On the day before the funeral, singer Harry Belafonte quietly approached Coretta and asked if she would consider going to Memphis to lead the march in Martin's place. Coretta did not hesitate. Taking the two oldest children with her, she flew to Memphis where she led the march to City Hall along with Ralph Abernathy, in support of the Sanitation Worker's Union. As crowds lined the streets, heads bowed in silence, the young widow moved between them with the dignity and composure that had become her public image, no matter what she felt inside. Through all the days of grief and despair, no one besides her own family, ever saw Coretta Scott King cry.

On Tuesday, April 9, 1968, Martin's funeral was held at the church where he had preached for many years. A hundred fifty thousand people had come to pay their respects, but the church could only accommodate seven hundred fifty. Coretta felt bad about this but when she came out of the church and saw tens of thousands of people standing in the streets where they had been listening to the service over the loudspeakers, she was deeply touched. As the crowds followed the family from the church to Martin's school, Morehouse College, Coretta realized this was her husband's last march. She was deeply grateful that even in death, "Martin was leading one of the greatest marches ever held."

After a brief, dignified service Martin was buried in South View Cemetery in Atlanta. Upon the crypt was carved the dead leader's triumphant words, "Free At Last, Free At Last! Thank God Almighty, I'm Free At Last."

Soon, the speeches, the visits, and the gifts of condolence were over. Now Coretta found herself plunged into a world she had never anticipated. Before her husband's death she had been his partner, ready and willing to share in his efforts for the cause in which they both believed. Now Coretta had a different role. She realized that the world was looking to her to go on from where the slain leader had abruptly left off -- and she was ready.

A few weeks after the funeral, the Poor People's Campaign was held in Washington, D. C. As the new leader of the SCLC, Ralph Abernathy led a group of individuals representing poor people from different areas around the country. The purpose of the campaign was to urge the government to promote jobs and a guaranteed annual income. During the first week of May, 1968, nine caravans of poor men and women arrived in Washington, D.C., and erected a camp of tents called Resurrection City.

Because it rained almost continually that week fewer people participated in the protest than the SCLC had expected. On the last day of the program, Coretta stepped up to the microphone and made a forceful speech denouncing violence as a "madness" that would destroy society unless it stopped. She called on women to draw on their resources of inner strength and form "a solid block of woman power" to help with the problems of the world. Fifty thousand women and men gathered near the Lincoln Memorial reacted to Coretta's strong words with resounding cheers and applause.

While Martin's widow was intent on furthering his goals, at the same time she had to cope with the practical realities of life, such as supporting her four children. Few people were aware of the King's financial problems, but the fact was that Martin had not planned for his children's educational future or their support. The small savings account and the one insurance policy he did have was of some help, but they did not provide a regular source of income. Many articles were being written about Coretta in various publications, and she received several honorary degrees, but they did not offer the needed financial security. At a Memorial Day concert in honor of Martin, Coretta narrated *Lincoln's Portrait*, a musical piece by Aaron Copeland. Though she was invited to repeat the performance with the Washington National Symphony, there was no provision for the financial remuneration that would have been helpful.

When Holt, Rinehart and Winston, a large New York publishing company, offered Mrs. King a substantial contract to write her autobiography, Coretta accepted and immediately got started, turning her bedroom into an office so she could be near the children while she worked. Coretta dictated the material for her book into a tape recorder.

In 1969, *My Life With Martin Luther King Jr.* was published and received generally favorable reviews. Some critics felt that the author had not revealed really personal things about Martin and herself, but that had not been her purpose. In the same way she conducted her life, Coretta's writing was dignified, restrained, and loyal to her husband's memory. The autobiography was translated into several languages, and the royalties helped to support the children's education and other important expenses.

When Martin's murderer -- a white man named Earl Ray, was brought to trial, Coretta did not appear in the courtroom. She did not want him to receive the death penalty because revenge was not part of her nature. When Ray pleaded guilty and was sentenced to life in prison, whatever she thought, she made no comment to the press. Though an assassin's bullet had ended Martin's life on earth, she knew it had failed in its purpose because the great leader's message was still alive.

On January 15, 1969, Martin's birthday, Coretta made an announcement about something which was to become the most outstanding project of her life. With the contributions of money that came pouring in after his death, she decided to build a center dedicated to Martin's memory and his work for peace and equality. What she had in mind was more than a marble statue or tombstone. She believed that the appropriate kind of memorial had to be a structure involved with meaningful purpose and activity.

To start with, she organized a foundation to help establish the memorial. The foundation's board of directors included Senators Hugh Scott and Edward Kennedy, Ralph Abernathy, former Vice President Hubert Humphrey and Coretta. In the hope that President Richard Nixon would propose legislation to build a memorial park in Martin's honor, Coretta appealed to the president personally. At first President Nixon appeared enthusiastic but after he thought it over, he told Coretta he didn't think it was a good idea. Instead he offered to help with a private fund-raising event. He suggested that the foundation sell recordings of the White House birthday party for musician Duke Ellington. Since such an event might raise thousands of dollars, but not the estimated ten million that would be needed for the kind of memorial Coretta was planning, she did not accept the president's offer.

For many months after Martin's death, letters addressed to Coretta continued to arrive from different parts of the world. Most of them expressed sympathy and belief in the dead leader's goals. Some of the letter writers included checks and cash, while some, believing that Mrs. King was a wealthy woman asked her for financial assistance. With the help of half a dozen volunteers, Coretta tried to answer most of the mail she received.

One of the people who was a tremendous help to Coretta was her sister, Edythe. Though they had not lived near each other after their respective marriages, the sisters had always maintained a close and loving relationship. After the funeral, Edythe came from Pennsylvania where she had been an English teacher and stayed with Coretta to help with the children and the running of the home.

Needing more room, Coretta set up an office in the basement of the house where she and a staff of five secretaries worked side by side. Coretta also hired a cook and a handyman to take care of chores so that nothing or no one would be neglected while she was occupied with her many demands. As more and more invitations to speak at universities, conferences, and churches continued to arrive, Coretta found herself involved in a schedule that took up every moment of her waking time.

When Coretta was elected to serve on the board of the SCLC, she discovered that the position was more of an honorary one than anything else. A small salary went along with the appointment but she did not feel comfortable in the organization's offices or with any of the new leaders. Though Coretta was not included in any policy making decisions, she agreed to make speeches whenever she was called on.

One very special request to speak came in the form of an invitation from St. Paul's Cathedral in London. In 1964 on his way to Norway to receive the Nobel Peace Prize, Martin had preached a sermon in the same cathedral, and the memory was still fresh in Coretta's mind. Now she, Martin's wife and co-worker, would be the first woman in history to address an audience from the same pulpit. It was a great honor for Coretta Scott King, as well as her family.

On March 14, 1969, Coretta and her four children flew to England. At the London airport they were surrounded by photographers, TV cameramen and reporters. Coretta did her best to smile, pose for pictures and answer questions, at the same time she tried to move her little family on to the hotel where they were staying. On Sunday, at St. Paul's Cathedral, Coretta's message to the audience was warmly received. The following day she spoke at Westminister Abbey. Again, her speech was a great success.

Very much like Martin, everywhere Coretta appeared, audiences came to listen and left impressed. Whenever she spoke, Coretta never failed to stress that she was continuing her husband's work, "to make all people truly free." As far as she was concerned, Coretta felt that Martin's message in death was even stronger than in life and she was there to prove it.

In 1969, Coretta used some of the funds she had been able to raise to buy property on Auburn Avenue in Atlanta for the Martin Luther King Jr. Center for Nonviolent Social Change. On January 14, 1970, a day before his birthday, Martin's body was moved to a permanent resting place in a marble crypt dedicated to his memory. It took many years of planning, speeches, and fund-raising to complete the beautiful complex as Coretta had planned.

In 1976 President Jimmy Carter helped the Center raise three and a half million dollars in federal construction funds. Another $4.7 million was raised from private business and labor foundations, including the Ford Motor Company. Slowly but surely one building after another rose and took on added purpose and meaning for the Center. Beside the elevated marble crypt, surrounded by a rectangular reflecting pool burns the Eternal Flame. Under a graceful archway a Freedom Walkway runs parallel to the pool. An all faiths chapel stands at one end of the complex while a three story building at the other end houses administrative offices, the King Library and Archives, a museum, a theater, a gift shop and an auditorium. With a generous donation from the national chapter of the Alpha Kappa sorority, the home on Auburn Avenue where Martin was born was also renovated and opened to visitors.

Admission to the center is free to the more than a half million visitors who come every year. The center is supported by city, state, and federal government foundations and individuals. Programs have been organized by the Center to educate people in the ideals of peace, nonviolence and civil rights. Classes are also conducted for those who are interested in learning about Martin's methods of solving problems nonviolently. In 1974 a student internship program was created which invited college students in this country and abroad for a semester of study at the King Center. More than twenty five young people learned how to work with community organizations and the principles of nonviolence.

During the Carter administration, Coretta was appointed as a member of the president's commission for the first National Women's Conference held in Texas. She was also chosen one of three public delegates to the 32nd General Assembly of the United Nations. Selected for their past contributions to society, Coretta, along with other delegates represented the United States at the United Nations General Assembly. Coretta was glad of the opportunity to renew her contacts with some of the African delegates. It was also an opportunity to discuss the ideas of nonviolence at the United Nations.

Along with her many activities and involvement with the Center, Coretta moved on to another important goal she had set for herself. By 1980, her four children were adults on their own. Now she was able to devote her energies wholeheartedly to making Martin's birthday celebrated officially as a national holiday.

Though President Carter had supported Coretta's goal, when he lost the 1980 election to Ronald Reagan, the new president was not interested. Not easily discouraged, Coretta went to Washington D. C. where she gathered signatures on petitions and spoke to important people in government circles. Among those who responded favorably were Senator Edward Kennedy, youngest brother of John Kennedy and a Democrat. When Republican Jack Kemp of New York was approached, he promised to solicit Republican votes to support the bill. Mr. Kemp was successful in keeping his promise.

It was a most rewarding achievement for Coretta when Martin's birthday was finally recognized as a national holiday. January 20, 1986, became the first federal holiday to honor a black American. After the ceremonial signing by President Reagan in the White House Rose Garden, reporters who were present questioned Coretta about the president's support of the bill, but she tactfully refrained from any comment.

The year 1986 presented other challenges to Coretta. In September she traveled to South Africa to lend her support in the struggle for equality by black people in that country. For the first time she met Winnie Mandela, the wife of activist Nelson Mandela, a man who had gone to jail for twenty years for his beliefs. Both women found their meeting meaningful because they had much in common. Coretta had hoped she might act as a peacemaker between the white government and the South African black people. But things did not work out because the political conflict was far more complicated than she had realized. However, she spent ten days in South Africa for the installation of Desmond Tutu as Anglican archbishop of Cape Town and met with many other black leaders.

On Coretta's return to America, she became involved in coordinating a march on Washington. This march focused on issues that were important to her, including world peace, joblessness, poverty and the downfall of the apartheid government in South Africa. Marching with Coretta were Jesse Jackson, SCLC president Rev. Joseph Lowery, NAACP Director Benjamin Hooks, Jr., and presidential candidate Governor Michael Dukakis. The day before the march, Coretta's

children, Marty and Bunny came to join the demonstration at the South African embassy in Washington. What
they were demonstrating against was the South African
government's policy of racial segregation known as
apartheid.

Mrs. King, her son and her daughter, along with
other protesters were arrested, handcuffed and jailed.
While many of the protesters were released hours later,
the King family chose to spend the night in prison. They
could not help feeling that Martin's spirit was there with
them.

While pursuing their own lives, Coretta's children
still managed to contribute to the King Center. Yolanda,
the oldest, had graduated from Smith College and spent
part of her time in Atlanta as director of Cultural
Affairs at the center. She also spoke at schools, drama-
tizing racial issues and trying to present solutions. Marty
became involved in politics as a commissioner in Fulton
County, Georgia, and worked as director of the Youth
Programs project at the center. Coretta's younger son,
Dexter, took charge of Special Events and Entertainment. For a while he also served as president of the
center with a goal that was "to tackle the center's daily
operations and mobilize the younger generation."
However, Coretta admitted to having difficulty in
sharing authority and in a few months she returned to
her former position as chief executive officer and
spokeswoman for the King Center.

In March, 1990, Coretta became involved with an
anniversary march in Selma, Alabama. It was the 25th
anniversary of the day that civil rights leaders marched
across the Pettus Bridge to demonstrate for the right of
black people to vote. On that day in 1965 there had
been much bloodshed and violence. In 1990, while

tension still existed, African Americans had earned the right to go to the polls and vote in every election.

In the 90's Coretta Scott King has not changed her commitment to the Cause. She refuses to alter her hopes and dreams regarding Martin's philosophy and the purpose of the King Center. On occasion Coretta has been criticized for not being "realistic" about today's problems in the black community. When some critics said that the Center was not really helping the poor, she responded that there has to be an institution to teach and promote the idea of nonviolence. "We are laying the foundation to train young leaders ... in the tradition of Martin Luther King. When you have enough world leaders who have been exposed this way, it'll make a difference."

While some impatient young black people consider her teaching to be outdated, Coretta persists in her vision, just as Martin did. Indicating increasing acts of racial violence as proof that her work will always be relevant, Coretta continues to talk to all those young people she is able to reach.

The King Center continues to teach Martin's principles of nonviolence. They include: accepting nonviolence as a way of life; trying to gain understanding through nonviolence; working to defeat injustice, not people; believing that "suffering can educate and transform people"; choosing love instead of hate; believing that "the universe is on the side of justice."

Workshops based on these six steps are taught at the Center to a variety of students of all ages and backgrounds. Trainees often include police officers, teachers and institutional leaders who are representatives of American organizations and companies in South Africa. Coretta's youngest daughter, Bernice, who had doctoral degrees in law and divinity, administered the King principles to students at the Center. Yolanda King organized a series of summer outdoor entertainment programs called Kingfests which attracted thousands of visitors to the Atlanta area.

Busy as her schedule is, Coretta manages to appear at many of the Center's activities. Nevertheless since her major priorities are to keep Martin's message alive and insure a steady income for the King Center, it is also necessary to continue traveling and speaking to audiences in this country and abroad. In 1990 when she returned to South Africa she met again with the Mandelas. Nelson Mandela had just been released from prison and Coretta invited the couple to visit when they came to the United States. During the summer the Mandelas came to Atlanta and Coretta mobilized the entire city in a celebration in their honor.

After her husband's untimely death the eyes of the world were on Coretta mostly in sympathy and mourning. Coretta responded with gentle dignity but she had no intention of remaining the silent widow of a great leader. Sincerely believing in what Martin lived and died for, in the years that followed, she emerged as her own person, strong and committed to the Cause she will not allow to be forgotten.

Back in 1952, a young woman met a young man with a "dream." Together they shared a long, frustrating struggle, making sacrifices, raising a family, and coping with tragedy without losing faith in their belief or themselves. While there has been criticism of Coretta Scott King, it does not deter her because she knows what she is doing is right. As a woman, she may have sacrificed a few private dreams of her own, but they are part of the past. Keeping her vision alive, of a just and peace-filled future for people everywhere, is what matters most to this lady.

No history of the Civil Rights Movement in America can be complete without the names of Martin Luther King, Jr., who led the way, and Coretta Scott King, who continues to move on with the dream into the 21st century.

EPILOGUE

In 1995, Dexter Scott King succeeded his mother as president and chief executive officer of the King Center. King Week, celebrated every year in January in the city of Atlanta, includes church services, public interest hearings, a special YMCA forum, and a teach-in which encourages parents and teachers to share ideas about incorporating Dr. King's philosophies in the schools. During the week, there is a National Parade of Celebration, complete with bands, floats, and people from across the nation. This popular event culminates with the National Martin Luther King, Jr. Holiday on January 15th. In 1977, Dexter King plans to build a $40 million interactive museum that would bring his father's teachings to life through use of computer technology.

At the Ebenezer Baptist Church, once the pulpit of Dr. King himself, Coretta Scott King delivers her State of the Dream Address. In memory of the original Civil Rights marches of three decades ago, there is a National March of Celebration that concludes with a rally in front of the King Center.

In 1993, a revised edition of Mrs. King's book, *My Life With Martin Luther King, Jr.* was published, and followed in 1994 by a paperback version. The brief but moving introduction by Coretta's family states that they are proud to be not only the sons and daughters of Martin Luther King, Jr. but equally proud to be the offspring of a woman like Coretta Scott King.

No one who has followed the inspiring life and career of this extraordinary Civil Rights activist can wonder why Yolanda, Martin, Dexter and Bernice feel the way they do. As she approaches the age of seventy, Coretta Scott King is planning to write another book, the title of which will probably be *My Life After Martin*. It will cover her efforts to build the King Center, achieve respect in the male-dominated civil rights community, and the problems of raising four children by herself. When this book is published, it will be more than a sequel to Coretta's first best seller, *My Life With Martin Luther King, Jr.*.

It will be the meaningful chronicle of a fearless fighter for justice who has found a separate and special peace of her own.

MARTIN LUTHER KING MEMORIAL
(Courtesy Meteor Photo & Imaging).

IMPORTANT DATES

1927: The birth of Coretta Scott
1940: Coretta starts attending the Lincoln School
1942: The Scott's home is burned
1945 Coretta becomes a student at Antioch College
1948: Coretta's first recital
1951: Coretta is accepted at the New England Conservatory of Music
1952: Coretta meets Martin Luther King, Jr.
1953: Coretta and Martin get married.
1954: A bachelor of music degree is awarded to Coretta at the New England Conservatory
The Kings move to Montgomery, Alabama
1955: The King's first child, Yolanda, is born
The start of the Montgomery bus boycott
1956: The King's home is bombed.
Coretta raises money by singing at concerts
Segregation in Montgomery's buses is ruled unconstitutional (Nov. 13th)
1957: Southern Christian Leadership Conference (SCLC) is organized
The Kings accept an invitation to Ghana
A son, Martin Luther King III, is born
1958: Martin's first book, *Stride Toward Freedom* published.
Mentally disturbed woman stabs Martin when he appears at a book signing.
1959: Coretta and Martin visit India
The King family relocate to Atlanta, Ga.

1960:   Freedom rides and sit-ins get under way
        Martin's release from prison is arranged by
        Senator John Kennedy
        On November 8, 1960, Kennedy becomes presi-
        dent of the United States
1961:   The King's second son, Dexter, is born.
1962:   Coretta travels to Switzerland to attend the
        Disarmament Conference.
1963:   Youngest child, Bernice, is born.
        Martin sent to Birmingham prison and detained
        Coretta contacts President Kennedy; Martin is
        freed.
        Civil rights bill proposed by president.
        On August 28th, a new march on Washington is
        organized.
        On November 22, President Kennedy is assassi-
        nated.
1964:   Coretta raises money for SCLC with Freedom
        Concerts
        Nobel Peace Prize awarded to Martin
        President Johnson signs Civil Rights Act
1965:   March from Selma to Montgomery
        Coretta joins Martin on the march
        On August 6th, Voting Rights Bill is passed
1966   Coretta, Martin, and the children live in a slum
        area of Chicago for the summer
1967:   Both Coretta and Martin speak out against
        Vietnam
1968:   On April 4th, Martin is killed in a Memphis
        motel
        Coretta takes Martin's place in Washington to
        speak at the Poor People's Campaign
1969   Coretta begins to build the Martin Luther King,
        Jr. Center for Nonviolent Social Change

Coretta's book, *My Life With Martin Luther King, Jr.* is published

1970: On January 14th, Martin's body is moved to the specially build crypt in the new center

1975: Martin's birthplace is renovated

1976: Jimmy Carter elected president of the United States

1977: Coretta continues work on Freedom Hall complex

Coretta receives appointment as delegate to the first National Women's

Conference in Texas; also becomes one of three delegates to the

United Nations General Assembly

1983: Martin Luther King Jr. Day proclaimed a national holiday

1986: First national celebration of Martin Luther King Jr. Day

Coretta goes to South Africa

1988: Coretta leads 25th anniversary march on Washington

1989: Coretta leads anniversary march in Selma (March 4)

When son Dexter resigns as president of King Center, Coretta resumes her former position

Coretta returns to Africa; invites Nelson and Winnie Mandela to Atlanta

Organizes town celebration

1995: Dexter Scott King succeeds his mother as chair, president, and chief executive officer of the King Center

1996: Plans for Memorial Museum to Martin Luther King, Jr. get underway.

Quotations from:

My Life With Martin Luther King, Jr.

Chapter I
"You are just as good as anyone else. You get an education and try to be somebody. Then you won't have to be kicked around by anybody, and you won't have to depend on anyone for your livelihood."

Chapter II
"There are some good white folks."

Chapter III
"Of course you're different, Corrie."

Chapter IV
"You have everything I ever wanted in a wife. There are only four things and you have them all."

Chapter V
"I don't mind. Somebody has to do it, and if you think I can, I will serve."

"You know that whatever you do, you have my backing."

Chapter VI
(February 1957, *Time magazine*: "The scholarly Negro Baptist minister who in little more than a

year has risen from nowhere to become one of the nations remarkable leaders of men."

"The time has come when I should no longer accept bail. If I commit a crime in the name of civil rights, I will go to jail and serve the time."
From *C. S. King Autobiography*: "As you well know," said Dr. Maynard, "your husband is an extraordinary man."

Chapter VII
"I would have talked about the women of India had I realized how much progress they had made with the coming of independence."

"Thankful that the spirit has guided me on this occasion."

"Why does Daddy have to go to jail?"

Chapter VIII
"I believe a hundred thousand people would come to the nation's capital at your invitation."

"This is what is going to happen to me, also."

"I think that Jesse Jackson and Operation Breadbasket have something that is needed in every community."

"If any of you are around when I have to meet my day, I don't want a long funeral."

"Mrs. King, I have been asked to tell you, Dr. King is dead."

Chapter IX

"Should I hate the man who killed my daddy?"
"No, darling, your daddy wouldn't want you to do that."

"Martin was leading one of the greatest marches every held."

"To tackle the center's daily operations and mobilize the younger generation."

"We are laying the foundation to train young leaders...in the tradition of Martin Luther King, Jr. When you have enough world leaders who have been exposed this way, it'll make a difference.

BIBLIOGRAPHY

BOOKS:

Saline, Carol *Sisters* Philadelphia, PA. (Photographs by Wohlmuth, Sharon) Running Press, 1994

King, Coretta Scott *My Life With Martin Luther King, Jr.* Rev. Ed. New York: Henry Holt & Co., 1993

Branch, Taylor *Parting the Waters: America in the King Years, 1954-63*, New York: Simon & Schuster, 1988

Patterson, Lillie *Martin Luther King, Jr. and the Freedom Movement*, New York: Facts on File 1989

King, Martin Luther King, Jr. *To the Mountaintop*, New York: Doubleday & Co., 1985

King, Coretta Scott *My Life With Martin Luther King, Jr.*, Holt, Rinehart & Winston, New York 1969

PERIODICALS:

Norment, Lynn "Coretta Scott King: the Woman Behind the King Anniversary" *Ebony*, January, 1990

Garland, Phyl "Coretta King: In Her Husband's Footsteps" *Ebony*, September 1968

Sanders, Charles L. "Finally I've Begun To Live Again." *Ebony*, November 1970

"The Widows: Keeper of the Dream" *Newsweek*, March 24, 1969

Williams, Juan "Coretta's Way" *Washington Post Magazine*, June 4, 1989

"Coretta King Urges World Peace on King's Birthday" *Jet*, October 4, 1985

Coretta Scott King, "1990-2035: 45 Years from Today" *Ebony*, November 1990

Walker, Alice "The Growing Strength of Coretta King" *Redbook*, September 1971

Coretta Scott King at Podium
New England Conservatory of Music Commencement
(Courtesy, Conservatory--photo by Frederick G.S. Clow)

Coretta being congratulated by Arthur Fiedler,
the famed Boston Pops Maestro
(Photo, Courtesy of Conservatory)

Coretta with children at Podium
(Photo, Courtesy of Conservatory)

INDEX